ETHAN ALLEN

&

THE CAPTURE OF
FORT TICONDEROGA

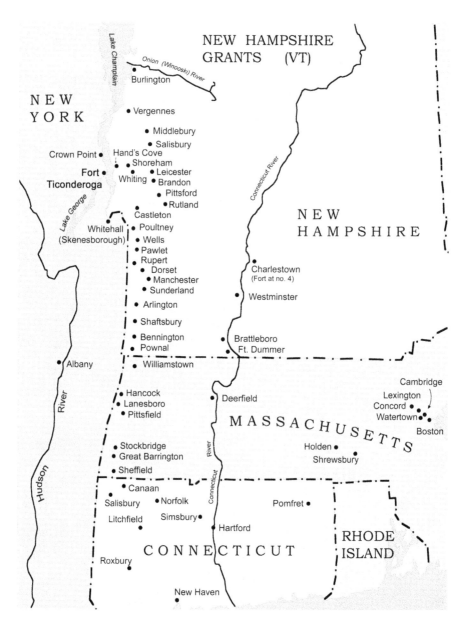

Selected towns involved in the capture of Fort Ticonderoga.

ETHAN ALLEN

& THE CAPTURE OF

FORT TICONDEROGA

RICHARD B. SMITH

THE
History
PRESS

Published by The History Press
Charleston, SC 29403
www.historypress.net

Cover images: Front: *"Allen needs you at Ti."* Reprinted by permission of National Life Group.
Artwork by Herbert M. Scoops. First published in the *Saturday Evening Post* and *Time*, 1947.
The illustration protrays a Green Mountain Boy recruiting another Green Mountain
Boy, as well as the clothing and armaments of the Boys at the time of the capture of Fort
Ticonderoga, May 10, 1775; "Fort Ticonderoga, New York." Photo by Nathan Farb. *Courtesy
of Fort Ticonderoga.* In the distance looking east beyond Fort Ticonderoga and Lake Champlain
is Vermont; *Map of Crown Point Road in 1759. Courtesy of the Crown Point Road Association.* Back:
Green Mountain Boy statue, Rutland, Vermont. Photo by Perez Ehrich. *Courtesy of Perez Ehrich;*
1955 Fort Ticonderoga Commemorative Stamp, U.S. Government Stamp. Portrays the four-
bastion star-shaped construction of Fort Ticonderoga with Ethan Allen in the foreground;
Salisbury furnace, Salisbury, Connecticut. *Courtesy of Ronald D. Jones, Salisbury, Connecticut.*
Portrays Ethan Allen's blast furnace as it was in 1763 at the time of his part ownership.

First published 2010
Second printing 2011
Third printing 2012
Fourth printing 2012
Fifth printing 2014

ISBN 9781540224057

Smith, Richard B.
Ethan Allen and the capture of Fort Ticonderoga : America's first victory / Richard Smith.
p. cm.
Includes bibliographical references and index.

1. Fort Ticonderoga (N.Y.)--Capture, 1775. 2. Allen, Ethan, 1738-1789. 3. Arnold,
Benedict, 1741-1801. I. Title.
E241.T5S658 2010
973.3'31--dc22
2010009530

Notice: The information in this book is true and complete to the best of our knowledge. It is
offered without guarantee on the part of the author or The History Press. The author and
The History Press disclaim all liability in connection with the use of this book.

Contents

CONTENTS

Acknowledgements

S everal individuals were helpful during the course of preparing this book by answering questions and providing information, manuscripts, artwork and books: Chris Fox, curator at the Fort Ticonderoga Association; Robert Maguire of Shoreham (Hand's Cove), Vermont; Paul Carnahan, librarian of the Vermont Historical Society Library in Barre, Vermont; Ron Jones of the Salisbury Association in Salisbury, Connecticut; Heather Harrington, assistant librarian at the Historic Deerfield Library; Brian Lindner of the National Life Group in Montpelier, Vermont; Don Martin of West Pawlet; Susanne Rapport, curator of the Dorset Historical Society; Jim Purdy, Elaine Purdy and Jim Rowe of the Crown Point Road Association; Joanna Jennings of the Sheffield Historical Society; Grace Simonds, Whiting town clerk; Reverend Billy Jones of the Whiting Community Church; Charles Sullivan of the Cambridge Historical Commission; Don Sutton, Ten Hen Studio and Nancy Finlay of the Connecticut Historical Society; Carol Bosco Baumann of the Red Lion Inn in Stockbridge, Massachusetts; Catherine Bermon of the Simsbury Historical Society in Simsbury, Connecticut; Holly Hitchcock and Claire Burditt of the Castleton Historical Society; Jeremy Dibbell of the Massachusetts Historical Society; Barry Whitney of Salisbury, Vermont; Joyce Kelley and Robert Childs of the Edmund Fowle House in Watertown, Massachusetts; and a special thanks to Perez Ehrich, who provided photographic help and photos as indicated. I would also like to acknowledge those who assisted with my previous book, from which I drew some information for this book.

ACKNOWLEDGEMENTS

Several historical societies and institutions were quite helpful. Some of those were the Vermont Historical Commission, the Connecticut Historical Society, the Massachusetts Historical Society, the Cambridge Historical Society, the Manchester Historical Society (Vermont), the Dorset Historical Society, the Sheffield Historical Society, the Simsbury Historical Society, the Pawlet Historical Society, the Castleton Historical Society, the Salisbury Association, the Crown Point Road Association and the Poultney Historical Society. The Bennington Museum and the Russell Collection in Arlington were also helpful.

I would also like to thank my wife, Sharon, for her great assistance and support. Her tour business has greatly increased my love and enjoyment of history.

Introduction

A merica's First Victory" was the May 10, 1775 surprise capture of Fort Ticonderoga. The story of this victory is not so much a military story as a story of freedom, land and people.

This is the story of citizen soldiers without uniforms, and some unarmed, going secretly into town after town to individually recruit patriots willing to risk almost everything to try to capture the massive "Gibraltar of the Americas," Fort Ticonderoga. The driving force was their dislike of tyranny—in some cases, tyranny of the land and in other cases, religious tyranny or overall tyranny of governments.

More recent information has allowed for the updating of accounts from the nineteenth and twentieth centuries of this dramatic event.

Part I

The Seeds and Forces of Rebellion Are Created

THINKING THE IMPOSSIBLE: CAPTURING FORT TICONDEROGA

The massive Fort Ticonderoga, which would become known as the "Gibraltar of the Americas," sits on a point high above Lake Champlain with over one hundred cannons and a star-shaped design that allows gunners to fire at any attacker from many directions. In 1758, 3,500 French defenders of Fort Ticonderoga held off about 16,000 attacking British soldiers.

Besides the physical size and design of the fort, colonial patriots in 1775 had to overcome many other obstacles, such as issues of command, lack of formal military training, lack of artillery or wall-scaling equipment and, in some cases, travel of more than two hundred miles—some from as far away as Connecticut. They had to recruit one by one in areas with small populations, get spies into the fort and keep the mission a secret yet march through land filled with many Tory (Loyalist) sympathizers. They had to obtain boats to cross Lake Champlain itself, worry about reinforcements from Canada and risk the possibility of losing their own land even if they won. How Fort Ticonderoga was captured by fewer than three hundred citizen soldiers and the story of the people who had become so oppressed to even attempt this can be found in the history of settlement of the early American colonists.

TENSIONS BETWEEN THE FRENCH AND ENGLISH MOUNT

The French and British Struggle Leads to an Uninhabited Wilderness

Ever since such early explorers as France's Marquis de Champlain and England's Henry Hudson in 1609, the British and the French had been major forces in trying to stake a claim of a part of the east coast of North America. The line between the French and British interests in the Northeast was disputed, and there were conflicts. The French and Indians in the north had even raided as far south as Deerfield, Massachusetts, in 1704.

With all of the tension and fear of French and Indian raids, the area known today as Vermont was an unoccupied wilderness located between the French and the English in the south (Massachusetts and Connecticut), as no settlers dared live there. The claim on the area by the English colony of New York was based on the 1664 charter from Charles II to the Duke of York that argued that the Connecticut River was the eastern border of New York. About 1741, New Hampshire became a royal colony of its own, and the king appointed Benning Wentworth as the royal governor. Also at this time, the Crown ruled that the border of New Hampshire and Massachusetts was farther south by a few miles than it was previously. This meant that Fort Dummer—which had been built west of the Connecticut River in today's Brattleboro area in 1743 to protect Massachusetts from French and Indian raids—was no longer in Massachusetts. The Crown gave responsibility for Fort Dummer to New Hampshire and not New York. Based on his new responsibility for Fort Dummer and on many other vague justifications, Benning Wentworth claimed that he could grant land and charter towns all the way to a boundary twenty miles east of the Hudson River.

Hence, in 1749, Benning Wentworth chartered the first of many towns west of the Connecticut River and called it Bennington. Although the New York royal governor objected, Wentworth chartered fifteen more towns (all were about six by six miles in size) before stopping in 1755 when the French and Indian War was about to begin. Of course, these were "paper" towns because no settlers dared to go there because of French and Indian raids.

The French Build Fort Carillon (Fort Ticonderoga)

To counter the British building a fort at the southern end of Lake George, the French started construction in 1755 of a fort fifteen miles south of their

FORT TICONDEROGA, TICONDEROGA, NEW YORK. Today's Fort Ticonderoga is shown with Vermont in the background and Lake Champlain looping around the peninsula. *Photo by Nathan Farb. Courtesy Fort Ticonderoga.*

own Fort St. Frederic at Crown Point on Lake Champlain. This new fort on Lake Champlain was initially called Fort Vaudreuil but was referred to later as Fort Carillon (later still to become Fort Ticonderoga). Construction of Fort Carillon took three years.

The location of the new fort was chosen carefully. It was sited at a narrow point on Lake Champlain so that artillery from the fort could hit vessels trying to travel north or south on Lake Champlain, thereby guarding the natural trade route from Canada south to Albany and New York City. It also would guard the three-mile portage route between Lake George and Lake Champlain where the Lake George waters flow into Lake Champlain.

The fort itself is located on a cliff, which would make an assault from the south difficult. Fort Carillon was designed to protect against forces moving north (i.e. the English). The chief designer was Marquis di Lotbiniere, who built it in the four-bastion star style of Maréchal de Vauban. The star shape allowed for deadly crossfire shooting if any troops attempted to attack. Over the next twenty years, the fort would be in many states of repair. Originally a log construction, it was reinforced in many places with stone.

The original four-sided fort had four star-shaped "bastions" added, and then two demilunes (walled triangle structures) were placed to the west and north and connected to the main fort by wooden bridges. These latter fortifications alone demonstrate the desire to thwart a ground attack that would most likely come directly into the fort from the north or the west but not from around the fort from the south. The southern wall between the fort and the lake was eventually stone. It was designed for a permanent garrison of four hundred men but was supplemented with some forces camping outside. It would have two to four thousand French troops during the summer.

Two years after the start of the French and Indian War, the British, to counter the southern movement and raids of the French, moved north in July 1758 under General Abercrombie to attack the French at Fort Carillon. In a massive, bloody battle on July 8, the British were defeated even though they had overwhelming forces (16,000 British to 3,500 French defenders).

The following year, 1759, the British under Jeffery Amherst attacked again, but the French merely evacuated Fort Carillon, blowing up the magazine and doing the same to the fort at Crown Point as they retreated to Canada. The British changed the name of Fort Carillon to Fort Ticonderoga.

British Build a Road and the War Ends

While the French were retreating to Canada, repairs were made to Fort Ticonderoga, and Jeffery Amherst decided in 1759 to build a military road running from the Fort at Number 4 (modern day Charlestown in New Hampshire) to the narrows at Crown Point northwest diagonally across the current state of Vermont. This would allow for bringing men and matériel to the Champlain Valley from Boston and the Atlantic Ocean and help to pursue the British attack on the French in Canada. Although its route was changed in sections and had periods of improvement and disrepair, fifteen years later sections of this twenty-foot-wide road would be used by the colonial patriots in the recapture of Fort Ticonderoga.

The road supported the British, who on September 13, 1759, defeated the French at Quebec. Then, one year later on September 8, 1760, Montreal surrendered, thus ending the North American portion (the French and Indian War) of the Seven Years' War. Although the final peace treaty, the Treaty of Paris, was not signed until 1763, it was clear that the French had been driven from North America when both Quebec and Montreal fell, in 1759 and 1760, respectively.

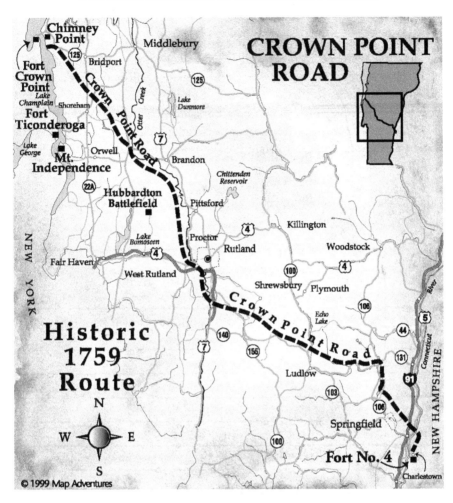

CROWN POINT ROAD. Crown Point Road was built by the British in 1759 to get supplies from the Connecticut River to Lake Champlain in order to help the British in their final push north to drive the French from North America. It opened the area to settlement, and parts were used in the capture of Fort Ticonderoga. *Courtesy Crown Point Road Association.*

AFTER THE FRENCH AND INDIAN WAR: 1760–1769

Although happy that they won, the British national debt swelled almost five times because of the war—from £30 million in 1753 to £140 million in 1763. The British started to demand that the colonists pay more toward this debt. At first, the colonists were jubilant that the war was over and new land was available.

In the 1730s and 1740s, the Connecticut legislature was beginning to open up the "upper towns" in northwest Connecticut on the east and west side of the Housatonic: Cornwall, Canaan, Sharon and Salisbury. To encourage settlement, inexpensive "rights" were sold. Similarly, an expansion was taking place north in western Massachusetts. Berkshire County was established in 1761, and nine new towns were organized in the 1760s, including Pittsfield, Great Barrington, Williamstown and Lanesboro. Sheffield had already been organized in 1733.

Table 1. Towns chartered under New Hampshire and New York grants west of Connecticut River in what is today Vermont.

Year	Number of New Hampshire towns chartered	Comments
1749	1	First New Hampshire town: Bennington in southwest Vermont
1750	1	
1751	2	
1752	2	
1753	7	
1754	3	English and French fighting accelerates
1755–58	0	
1759	0	French and Indian War effectively ends
1760	1	Settlers really begin to come to Vermont
1761	61	
1762	10	
1763	35	
1764	5	June: New Hampshire makes last full town grant (Hubbardton)
		July: Crown rules Connecticut River "to be" the eastern border of New York
1765–75		New York charters over one hundred towns, many overlapping existing Grants towns

The Seeds and Forces of Rebellion Are Created

Farther to the north, the vacant, untamed wilderness now known as Vermont was opened to settlement in 1760. Benning Wentworth made incredibly cheap land available to settlers from Connecticut and Massachusetts. Because of the shaky legal status vis-à-vis New York's claims, some lands were sold for one four-hundredth of the value of equivalent land in other areas such as western Massachusetts. Wentworth turned aggressive in 1761, and by 1764 he had chartered over 125 towns. Some towns were regranted, and there were some military grants as well; the trend was clear, as shown in Table 1. The area became known as the "New Hampshire Grants," or simply the "Grants," and is today Vermont.

The Privy Council Ruling of 1764 Rules in Favor of New York

In 1764, fifteen years after the first charter was granted to the town of Bennington from New Hampshire, the British Privy Council ruled that the line between New York and New Hampshire was "to be" the western shore of the Connecticut River. Unfortunately, the Crown used the words "to be." The ruling didn't indicate the status of the current landowners and settlers who had already bought land in the more than 125 towns in the "New Hampshire Grants."

The Crown Rules: The Proclamation of 1763

Another ruling about the same time made colonists unhappy from Georgia to New England. The Crown issued the Proclamation of 1763, which noted that settlement north or west of the headwaters of rivers flowing into the Atlantic were off-limits to settlers. The stated purpose was to keep the Native Americans happy. The colonists felt that this was an excuse to keep them hemmed into the Atlantic seaboard and hence easier to regulate. This was the beginning of a growing resentment. The proclamation was never truly followed (even George Washington took exception); it was the beginning of more than ten years of attempts by the Crown to limit geographical freedom, to get cheap land and to limit freedom of the colonists.

Disputes with the Crown and New York Grow-Year by Year

The Proclamation of 1763 started a long battle between the colonists and England. To pay for debts, the Crown imposed the Sugar Act and the Currency Act in 1764. In 1765, there was the Stamp Act and the Quartering Act. In 1766, there was the Declaratory Act, and in 1767, the

PROCLAMATION OF 1763. At the end of the French and Indian War, the Crown restricted the original thirteen colonies to settlement only as far inland as the headwaters of rivers flowing to the Atlantic Ocean. Although not generally followed, it was the beginning of the Crown's restrictive measures on the colonists. Fort Ticonderoga is shown with a dot. *Based on maps in* National Atlas of the United States.

Townshend Acts. All involved more taxes and more restrictions on the colonists' freedoms.

Resistance and tensions started to grow. British troops were harassed and houses looted. Boycotts were encouraged and used. Refusal to follow the king's rulings on quartering was frequent. More laws and more boycotts followed. Courts were dissolved in some states. Customs officials were locked up. Residents were urged to arm themselves. Threats were made to send agitators to trial in England instead of in the colonies. In 1764, Committees of Correspondence were organized by Samuel Adams in Massachusetts to spread information and propaganda. In July 1765, the Sons of Liberty groups were formed in many towns in the colonies to resist these acts and laws. These underground organizations used violence, physical force and intimidation. In 1765, the Sons and Daughters of Liberty started to fight back, often taking law into their own hands via tarring and feathering.

In the Grants, the New York government interpreted the Crown's 1764 ruling as giving New York the right to issue its own land grants and make those on the land pay for the same land again. New York started in earnest to sell land in Vermont. A peaceful delegation led by Bennington's Samuel Robinson convinced the English to demand that New York stop issuing charters until the Crown's wishes were known. New York ignored the Crown's ruling. From 1765 until 1775, the New York government issued over one hundred land patents (i.e. town charters) in what is now Vermont. Many of these towns overlapped the already-granted New Hampshire towns.

GREEN MOUNTAIN BOYS AND SONS OF LIBERTY

Ethan Allen Takes Charge in 1770

Some New Hampshire Grants proprietors agreed to a peaceful solution via a trial in Albany, New York, that would determine which of two conflicting land claims in Shaftsbury were valid. This trial was part of the test known as the Ejectment Trials. If the court ruled for New York, proprietors on New Hampshire lands worried that they would have to pay New York again for the same land.

These proprietors met in Salisbury, Connecticut, and asked Ethan Allen to lead and organize the fight with New York at the trials. They had the right man. Ethan was familiar with the Grants. Leaving his family in Sheffield, Massachusetts, he had moved to Bennington. His cousins from Roxbury, Connecticut, had already moved to the Grants: Seth Warner to Bennington in 1763 and his other cousin, Remember Baker, to Arlington in 1764. At the time he was asked to lead the fight, Allen did not own land in the Grants, but that would change very quickly.

Allen was a six-foot-tall, flamboyant, freedom-loving leader. He was honest yet fallible. He liked to drink with his friends and was a good organizer. Although not college educated, he was good with the written and spoken word. People liked having him around. He was also a large and strong man, capable of being domineering. He rebelled against accepted dogma and any authority. His religious views as a deist were confusing. Many years later, George Washington would describe Allen by saying, "There is an original something about him that commands admiration."

Ethan's father had bought "rights" to cheap land in Cornwall when the Connecticut legislature opened up northwest Connecticut. Ethan had five brothers and two sisters (Heman, born 1740; Lydia, born 1742; Heber, born 1743; Levi, born 1745; Lucy, born 1747; Zimri, born circa 1748; and Ira, born 1751)—all with the same spirit. After his father died when Allen was seventeen, which put a stop to his hope of going to Yale, he became involved with a variety of entrepreneurial ventures. Ethan moved to Salisbury, Connecticut, when he was twenty-three.

Surprisingly, the beautiful Salisbury of today had vast iron ore deposits, but there was a need for a blast furnace in those days. Ethan Allen had gone into partnership in 1762 with his brother Heman and John Hazeltine to build a blast furnace in Salisbury in an area known as Furnace Village (now Lakeville). Ethan didn't know it at the time, but John Hazeltine would move to Vermont and play a role in Vermont's east-side towns such as Chester and Westminster. Paul became opposed to the tyranny of the Crown. No small, unimportant venture, this was the first blast furnace in northwest Connecticut and would eventually produce the ore for more than eight hundred cannons during the Revolution.

SALISBURY FURNACE, CIRCA 1763, SALISBURY, CONNECTICUT. Started in 1762 by Ethan Allen, John Hazeltine and others, the first blast furnace in northwest Connecticut eventually produced about 42 percent of the cannons used by the colonists in the Revolutionary War (including those captured from the British and supplied by France and Spain). *Courtesy Ronald D. Jones, Salisbury, Connecticut.*

The Seeds and Forces of Rebellion Are Created

Allen married Mary Brownson, and in 1764 he sold his half interest in the Cornwall family farm and then half of his ironworks share to his brother Heman, who moved to Salisbury and managed a general store until his death in 1778. In 1765, Allen sold his remaining share. During his Salisbury days, Ethan had also become involved with religious issues. He had been in contact with Dr. Thomas Young, who would encourage Ethan's seeds of religious independence, his becoming a deist and his generally being a lover of liberty. (As a side note, it was Dr. Young who would later be credited by many for coining the word "Vermont" for the "Grants.")

After Salisbury, Ethan's venturesome spirit got him involved with a lead-making operation in Northampton, Massachusetts. After then moving to Sheffield, Massachusetts (about six miles north of Salisbury), in 1767, he spent a lot time in the Grants, hunting and trapping for furs to put in Heman's store and ended up moving to Bennington in 1769.

Taking action immediately in February 1770, Allen went to New Hampshire to get the land documents, stopped in New Haven, Connecticut, to get another lawyer and then went on to Albany, stopping off in Sheffield to see his family. Armed with two lawyers, he arrived in Albany in June 1770. New York attorney general John Tabor Kemp and James "Swivel Eyes" Duane represented New York claimants. The presiding judge and the New York lawyers all owned land under New York patents in the Grants. Before the trial had even really begun, the judge ruled that the New Hampshire Grants were not valid. When confronted after the results of the trial, Ethan Allen showed the fight in him. As Ira Allen said, he defiantly told the powerful lawyer for the New York patent holders:

The gods of the valleys are not gods of the hills.

When asked what that meant, Allen defiantly said, "Come to the Grants and I'll show you what I mean."

Allen returned to his house in Bennington from Albany to find the settlers mad. After doing the backbreaking work of clearing their land of trees and rocks, these farmers and hunters were not going to pay New York again for the land they had bought legally with the stamp of another royal governor, New Hampshire's Benning Wentworth. They didn't want to be subservient to the New York "patroon" system, which favored large landowners. They had come not only for cheap land but for freedom as well, from British tyranny as well as local tyranny. In many cases, they had

ETHAN ALLEN'S HOUSE, BENNINGTON, VERMONT. The house in the foreground has been attributed to Ethan Allen while he resided in Bennington from 1769 to 1775. The house and the courthouse behind it are no longer there, but Old First Church is still there today. The cemetery has been expanded to where the first two buildings are located today. A marker now indicates where the home was located. *Courtesy Vermont Historical Society.*

also come for religious freedom. The Great Awakening had many people leaving Connecticut and Massachusetts for more religious freedom. Many of the settlers were New Light Congregationalists, Separatists and New Side Presbyterians. The pro–New York side consisted of more Old lights and Anglicans.

Allen called for a "convention" to be held at the Fay's Tavern (later more widely known at the Catamount Tavern). Allen convinced the assemblage that force would be necessary not against the Crown but rather the New York government. New Hampshire had been washing its hands of the issue since the Crown's ruling in 1764. It was decided that they would organize, and Ethan Allen was elected colonel commandant, ensuring the beginnings of a paramilitary group. When the settlers started to resist, the governor of New York said that he would drive this group back into the Green Mountains—hence they started calling themselves the Green Mountain Boys. The less glamorous names given

CATAMOUNT TAVERN, BENNINGTON, VERMONT. Also known as Fay's Tavern and the Green Mountain Tavern, the Catamount Tavern served as the headquarters of the Green Mountain Boys. Ethan Allen left from here to capture Fort Ticonderoga in 1775. The tavern burned down in 1871. Calvin Dart may have taken the photo. *Courtesy Vermont Historical Society.*

later by the governor of New York would be "the Bennington Mob" or the "Bennington Rioters." The New York governors never really understood that a well-organized paramilitary group was being formed. In the following year, Nathaniel Spencer from Arlington, who later deserted and became a Tory, wrote, "One Ethan Allen hath brought from Connecticut twelve or fifteen of the most blackguard fellows he can get, double-armed, in order to protect him."

Allen organized at least five companies by territory (some more than fifty miles apart), with captains: Seth Warner (Allen's cousin) for Bennington; Remember Baker (Allen's cousin) for Arlington; Robert Cochran for Rupert; Gideon Warren for Sunderland and the vicinity, although he showed up at Hampton and Pownal as well; and Dr. Ebenezer Marvin (whose wife was born in Salisbury, Connecticut) for the Grants, although he moved to Stillwater, New York, in 1777. Matthew Lyon in Wallingford is also believed to have been a captain of the Green Mountain Boys. (All six of these "captains" had ties to Allen and would be with him at Ticonderoga.)

Green Mountain Boy Statue, Rutland, Vermont. The Green Mountain Boys wore no real uniforms at the beginning of the war and were basically farmers and woodsmen at the time of the capture of Fort Ticonderoga. The statue was dedicated in 1915 by the Ann Story chapter of the DAR. *Photo by Perez Ehrich. Courtesy Perez Ehrich.*

The Boys themselves were primarily farmers (more than 60 percent), and more than 70 percent owned land when they joined. About 43 percent originally came from Connecticut and another 40 percent, from Massachusetts. Most only had a basic education, and 39 percent were in their twenties. Having been born in 1738, Allen himself was about thirty-two when elected colonel commandant. The Green Mountain Boys were volunteers ready to defend their freedoms against the "Yorkers."

In total, there would have been about three hundred Green Mountain Boys, but there are some suspect claims of the number going as high as one thousand. Most of the Boys were concentrated along the western part of modern-day Vermont. They had no uniforms except for maybe a twig in their hat. Of course, Ethan Allen, being a little flashier, had an outfit with "fancy, gold-braided epaulettes" and a sword. Few other facts are known, but he did have and use a horse. Over time, state militia units, like modern-day National Guard units, would be referred to as the Green Mountain Boys.

The decision to use force by the Green Mountain Boys was not unusual and actually came late compared to other colonies. After forming about 1765, the Sons of Liberty and similar groups had become increasingly active in New England. There was concern that the British were going to "occupy" the colonies. This agitation resulted in the March 15, 1770 Boston Massacre, during which British soldiers fired on a crowd. However, there was a peaceful trial held in which the key British officer was found innocent. The Boston Massacre actually came before the formation of the Green Mountain Boys and the peaceful Ejectment Trials.

MORE RESISTANCE AND SETTLEMENT: 1770–1775

In 1770, the Grants had a very small relative population compared with other neighboring colonies as shown in the following:

Table 2. Population of the colonies in 1770 (total persons).

Vermont (the Grants)	10,000
New York	162,000
Massachusetts (including Plymouth and Maine populations of about 31,000 total)	235,300
Connecticut	183,900
New Hampshire	62,400
Rhode Island	58,200

Note: The total population of the colonies had reached over 2,200,000. Of the roughly 10,000 in the Grants, many lived on the eastern side near New Hampshire.

For the next five years, from the Catamount Tavern, Green Mountain Boys were dispatched up and down Vermont (primarily on the west side of the Grants) to harass and intimidate any settlers with "Yorker" titles. Although Allen had served in the French and Indian War, it was for only about fourteen days, so he would gain almost all of his guerrilla military skills from directing the Green Mountain Boys. The main tactics he learned were speedy reaction, secrecy and then surprise. In addition to surprise and speed, tactics perfected included spying, stealth, intelligence, communication, nighttime attacks and deception. They learned to travel over long distances secretly. Of course, by protecting the settlers, Allen acquired the unwavering support and loyalty of the farmers and people in the region.

There were almost monthly confrontations. For instance, in May 1771, word had reached Bennington that a New York surveyor was in the Pittsford, Vermont area (about sixty miles north of Bennington). Ethan Allen assembled some Green Mountain Boys and immediately rode to Pittsford. Intimidated, the surveyors left. Pittsford would return the loyalty by providing five men in the attack on Fort Ticonderoga four years later. In that same year, the high sheriff of Albany County, Ten Eych, had come toward Bennington, about thirty miles from Albany, with a posse of about three hundred men to eject James Breakenridge from his farm (a New Hampshire title). Through a network of spies and friends, word reached the New Hampshire Grants settlers. They armed themselves and then placed themselves in strategic places: houses, a field, on a ridge and so forth. Although outnumbered, the settlers were able to hold off the posse.

Another confrontation occurred when Ethan Allen, Remember Baker, Robert Cochran (all three would be at the capture of Ticonderoga) and six other Boys went to Rupert (thirty-five miles north of Bennington and on the road to Fort Ticonderoga) and burned a "Yorker" settler's house. They didn't kill the settler, but that sure comes close. Another act of force occurred when the Green Mountain Boys surprised a Yorker sympathizer, brought him to Bennington and hanged him by a chair in front of the Catamount Tavern until he mended his ways.

In 1772, New York actually put a bounty on the head of Ethan Allen, his cousin Remember Baker, Robert Cochran and several others. Thus the king's colony, in which Fort Ticonderoga sat, made Ethan Allen, Remember Baker and Robert Cochran subject to death if caught.

The oppressive power and size of New York's government did not intimidate the Green Mountain Boys. Three of the most brazen Green Mountain Boys, in turn, put out a reward themselves for the capture of James Duane and John Kemp. The willingness to sign this showed that Ethan Allen was ready to defy the mighty New York governor and stand up for the rights of all towns to the north in Vermont. Kemp was the New York attorney general, and James Duane (the lawyer at the Ejectment Trials) was no low-level player, either; Duane was chosen to be one of the seven delegates from New York to the first Continental Congress in 1774, with very sympathetic views toward the king. The reward was also appealing to the peasants and gathered loyal support for years:

The Seeds and Forces of Rebellion Are Created

£25 Reward

Whereas James Duane and John Kemp of New York, have by their menaces and threats greatly disturbed the public peace and repose of the honest peasants of Bennington and the settlements to the northward, which peasants are now and ever have been in the Peace of God and the King and patriotic and liege subjects of George III. Any person that will apprehend these common disturbers viz James Duane and John Kemp and bring them to Landlord Fays at Bennington, shall have £15 reward for James Duane and £10 for John Kemp paid.

Ethan Allen
Remember Baker
Robert Cochran
Dated Feb. 5 1772
Poultney

Another incident showing how quickly the Boys could react occurred in 1772. A New York sheriff went into the Arlington home of Remember Baker captured him and put him on a carriage to take him back to Albany. Baker's wife, Desire, escaped and woke up neighbors. Within an hour there were twelve people from the Bennington-Arlington area chasing the carriage to Albany. They caught up with the carriage in Troy, about thirty miles from Arlington but only a mile or so from Albany itself. They freed Remember, who returned to the Grants.

Even British troops didn't scare Ethan. In 1772, word reached Bennington that British troops were coming up the Hudson River with the New York governor to oust the New Hampshire settlers. Ethan Allen, using his growing military acumen, sent a spy (his younger brother Ira) into the Albany area to find out the facts. Although many of the settlers were reluctant to take on the British, Ethan Allen prevailed and drew up elaborate military-like plans to fight the British. As it turned out, the British were merely going to relieve some troops in the Niagara region of western New York.

On February 5, 1774, the General Assembly of New York issued a new resolution involving a reward of fifty pounds against eight Green Mountain Boys in the Grants: Ethan Allen, Seth Warner, Remember Baker, Robert Cochran, Peleg Sunderland, Silvanus Brown, James Breakenridge and John Smith. Of the eight people mentioned, five would be with the expedition fifteen months later to capture Fort Ticonderoga, which was located on the land of the New York colony that had issued the reward.

Amid these frequent confrontations, in 1772 Ira Allen had been surveying the lush valleys and rivers near Lake Champlain on the Onion River (now called the Winooski River) in the Burlington, Colchester and Winooski area today. Burlington and Colchester were both chartered on the same day in 1763. Both were granted to people from Salisbury, Connecticut, and these proprietors' meetings were in Salisbury, where Heman Allen still had a general store. The Allen brothers (Ethan, Ira, Heman and Zimri), along with Remember Baker, then formed in early 1773 the Onion River Land Company to purchase and develop land in the greater Burlington area. By May 1773, they already had forty-five thousand acres there. To protect themselves and potential settlers, Ira and Remember also built near the falls of the Onion River an armed blockhouse (with thirty-two portholes in the upper story). The second story jutted out so that water could be poured over

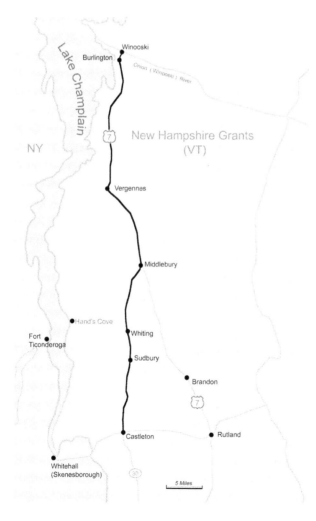

ONION RIVER LAND COMPANY ROAD. In 1773, Ira Allen and Remember Baker built a seventy-mile "road" from Castleton to the Burlington and Colchester area to open up settlement for their landholdings in the Onion (Winooski) River area. The Castleton-Whiting section of the road was used in 1775 to go to Hand's Cove.

the walls in case of attackers. The roof was detachable, so if it caught fire it could be thrown off.

More importantly, Ira and Remember, in the summer of 1773, built a seventy-mile-long "road" (more of a formal path) from Castleton to Burlington to facilitate getting to and from their vast holdings. Although primitive, it did serve the purpose. This road crossed the old east–west Crown Point Road in Sudbury. Two years hence, this road would form part of the route to Fort Ticonderoga. Having to travel to their landholdings in northern Vermont, the Allen clan became familiar with every nook and cranny of the region.

*Colonists in New England Fight the Crown
but Offer an Olive Branch*

After the Boston Massacre in March 1770, there were also many other incidents in New England, especially in Boston, of resistance to authority— in this case England rather than New York.

In 1772, colonists from Rhode Island set fire to a customs schooner in Narragansett Bay. Important Committees of Correspondence were set up to communicate between towns and other colonies. In 1773, on December 16, the Sons of Liberty protested British tea regulations and dumped tea into the Boston Harbor. One of the leaders of the participants was Thomas Young, Ethan Allen's friend and mentor when Ethan lived in Salisbury, Connecticut. In response, Parliament in March 1774 passed the first of several Coercive Acts (called the Intolerable acts by colonists). The Boston port bill effectively closed down all commercial shipping in Boston Harbor. The other acts included the Administration of Justice Act, the Massachusetts Government Act, the Quartering Act of 1774 and the Quebec Act. The last, also in 1774, among other features turned over rule of the western Indian reserves to Quebec, allowed French-based civil law for private matters and restored French system of land ownership. If war were to come, the British did not want the seventy thousand French Canadians to support the colonists.

From September 5 to October 26, 1774, the First Continental Congress met in Philadelphia with fifty-six delegates from all the colonies except Georgia. The Grants, as they were not Vermont proper yet, were not represented. In fact, New York sent James Duane, for whom Ethan Allen had set a reward, as a delegate. The Congress essentially ordered that the Intolerable Acts were "not to be obeyed." The rights of "life, liberty and property" were asserted. Although there was a call for boycotts of English imports and other measures, there still were present tones of conciliation and hope. In fact, the Continental Congress noted that the colonists should respect the king's property at Fort Ticonderoga and only use force in a defensive way.

The Second Continental Congress was scheduled to meet the following spring on May 10, 1775, in Philadelphia. Ironically, this would be the same day on which Fort Ticonderoga would be captured.

AT THE BEGINNING OF 1775

In the Grants, the violence continued but was still mainly directed against New York authority. Benjamin Hough, who had been appointed by New York to be a justice of the peace in Claredon, south of Rutland, was "arrested" by neighbors for being troublesome and was taken to the Tinmouth home of Colonel John Spafford, a native of Salisbury, Connecticut. On January 30, 1775, he was "tried" by seven judges: Ethan Allen, Seth Warner, Robert Cochran, Peleg Sunderland, James Mead, Gideon Warren and Jesse Sawyer. He was sentenced to two hundred lashes on the naked back (sometimes referred to as the "Beach Seal" because of the use of beach branches or as "Twigs of the Wilderness") and commanded to depart the Grants, never to return. These "judges" (except for Mead and Sawyer), plus the owner of the courthouse, John Spafford, would be with the expedition to capture Fort Ticonderoga less than three months away.

The Sons of Liberty had also become more physical—tarring and feathering, boarding ships and throwing tea into the water, burning ships and more. The Sons of Liberty with their Liberty Poles publicized their cause just as Ethan Allen had written many articles for the *Connecticut Courant* (predecessor of the *Hartford Courant*) to gain sympathy there. Also, like the Minutemen (usually part of state militias) in New England, the Green Mountain Boys could react on a moment's notice. The main difference between the Green Mountain Boys, the Sons of Liberty and the Minutemen was that the Green Mountain Boys had one centralized, unquestioned leader.

Connecticut foresaw the inevitable, and in December its General Assembly commissioned and paid for two independent military companies, organized two new military regiments and ordered artillery. The assembly ordered training by May 1, 1775. It would have more than 6,000 men in a peacetime colony with a population of little more than 183,000. By May, Connecticut had organized about twenty-eight militia regiments, then totaling about 23,000 men.

Perhaps because Ethan Allen witnessed both what Connecticut was doing and the greater issue of British tyranny, on March 1, 1775, from his family's home in Sheffield, Massachusetts, he wrote to Oliver Wolcott, the prominent Connecticut political and military figure who was going to be a delegate at the upcoming Continental Congress, scheduled to start on May 10 in Philadelphia:

> *Provided the Controversy between Great Britain and the Colonies Should Terminate in a War the Regiment of Green Mountain Boys Will I Dare Ingage to Assist their American Brethren in the Capacity of Rangers.*

The situation in the colony of New York was a mixed bag. Governor Tryon was personally popular, but he and Lieutenant Governor Cadwallader on balance favored the king. (Richard Ketchum's book, *Divided Loyalties*, covers these complex issues in pre–Revolutionary War New York.)

THE CROWN IGNORES WARNINGS ABOUT FORT TICONDEROGA

As early as 1767, British governor Carleton had said that "it is not only expedient but indispensably necessary" to keep the lake posts in repair. But over the years, upstate New York had been relatively quiet. Across the lake, in the Grants, there was only the "Bennington Mob," and they were small, not against the Crown necessarily and located eighty miles away in Bennington.

Elsewhere, in places like Massachusetts, however, the situation was getting so tense that on May 2, 1774, His Excellency Frederick Haldimand, Esq., a key British military leader, commanded John Montressor to examine the state of the forts at Crown Point and Ticonderoga. On May 13, Montressor reported that the "Fort at Ticonderoga is in ruinous situation" and "in many places there are very capital breaches." His report, however, was written in the context of having a fort that would "protect Navigation, Vessels, Storehouse, Wharves, Landings." There were no indications in that report that it, even in a ruinous condition, could not withstand an attack of a small force, such as five hundred to one thousand men. He did not, from a military point of view, state that if the cannons packed with grapeshot were lined up in front of the breaches they could not repel a ground attack from a small force.

Two days later, on May 15, Haldimand wrote Lord Dartmouth in England that he would propose to Thomas Gage, governor of Massachusetts, the drawing of two regiments from Canada to Crown Point "under the pretense of rebuilding that fort which from its situation not only secures the communication with Canada but also opens easy access to the back settlements of the Northern colonies and may keep them in awe." Apparently, neither Dartmouth nor Gage saw anything in the idea. Certainly they did not act with any speed.

Later in 1774, as tensions increased, there were many instances of the colonists trying to acquire arms. In September, the British military commander, Gage, seized the Massachusetts arsenal of weapons at Charlestown. On September 1, 1774, upon being informed that Massachusetts towns had been removing their gunpowder from the Provincial Powder House in Somerville—which held gunpowder belonging to both individual towns and provincial government—British troops seized the gunpowder.

On October 5, Thomas Gage sent a note to Captain Delaplace, who was the British commander of Fort Ticonderoga: "I am fully sensible of the bad state of the Buildings at Ticonderoga and am not surprised at the accident you mention, you did the right thing in ordering some small repairs, to make the Commissary's Room habitable but you will be at as little Expence as possible, as it may soon be expected something will be decided respecting that Fort."

On November 2, Lord Dartmouth in England wrote to Gage in Boston "to give the proper orders for putting" both Fort Ticonderoga and Crown Point "in such a State as may effectually answer the purposes for which they were originally intended." By the time Gage received the letter in December, winter had set in, and all action had to wait.

On December 5, 1774, Rhode Island ordered the powder and shot in Fort George removed to a place of safety. Another outbreak of violence involving the colonists trying to acquire arms occurred on December 14–15, 1774. Fort William and Mary, which guards the Portsmouth, New Hampshire harbor, had cannons and powder taken by a "mob" of about four hundred men.

On February 10, 1775, Captain Delaplace wrote about an incident. A single man wanted to buy powder from the fort and had asked about the strength of the fort and whether "sentries were planted at the gate" and afterward went away. The captain surmised that other men might want to seize the ammunition at Ticonderoga. Gage in Boston thought that this incident was not important. It could have been a hunter. Guy Carleton in Canada, because of various incidents, did eventually send reinforcements to Fort Ticonderoga in the form of Lieutenant Feltman and ten other men, but not until after April 12. They arrived between April 19 and May 10 but had not heard of events at Lexington and Concord. Further reinforcements were expected in early May to help rebuild the fort, but they would be delayed.

It should have been increasingly clear that the colonists were getting desperate for arms. On March 16, Gage, now governor of Massachusetts and commander in chief of all of His Majesty's forces in America, wrote to Carleton in Canada to send Lieutenant Marr to Crown Point (not even mentioning Fort Ticonderoga) to see if there were any objections to the plan regarding work on the forts or whether there was a better plan than rebuilding the fort. There was no sense of urgency to improve the defenses for this remote upstate New York fort, even with its more than one hundred cannons.

Finally, on April 15, 1775, Lord Dartmouth in England wrote to General Gage in Boston and ordered that "all" forts in North America (which included Canada) should be reinforced. The people hand-delivering the letter were on the ship *Cerberus*, which left from Portsmouth, England. The letter did not arrive until May 25, fifteen days after May 10, 1775 (the capture of Fort Ticonderoga). Gage, at the time of Lexington and Concord, had also intended to bring a large reinforcement to Fort Ticonderoga—the Seventh Regiment from Canada—but by the time the letter reached Carleton in Canada it was too late.

Importance of Fort Ticonderoga to Colonists

The colonists, if not the British, saw the real and immediate importance of Fort Ticonderoga both as source of arms and as a way to control the British from using Canada as a backdoor entry down Lake Champlain to split the colonies. The Massachusetts Committee of Correspondence (headed by Samuel Adams) sent John Brown of Pittsfield, Massachusetts, to Canada to get a feeling for which side Canada would take if there was a rebellion. Brown went to Canada with Green Mountain Boy Peleg Sunderland (Manchester), who was acquainted with the St. Francois Indians and their language. He was a friend of Ethan Allen's. Both Brown and Sunderland were at the capture of Fort Ticonderoga in May.

Brown's March 29, 1775 letter from Montreal to the Committee of Correspondence (sent to Samuel Adams and Dr. J. Warren in Cambridge) summarized his findings of a month-long trip to Canada. The Canadians would not send a representative to the upcoming May 10 Continental Congress since it was not clear they would support the colonists. Of major importance in this secret March 29 letter, written in Montreal, was his last statement (the non-italics are the author's for emphasis):

> *One thing I must mention, to be kept as a profound secret,* The Fort at Ticonderoga must be seized as soon as possible, *should hostilities be committed by the King's troops.* The people on New-Hampshire Grants have engaged to do this business, *and in my opinion they are the most proper persons for this job.* This will effectually curb this Province, and all the Troops that may be sent here.

The same letter also noted that "I have established a channel of Correspondence through the New Hampshire Grants which may be depended on." It was not clear who in the Grants actually said that they would "do this business."

FINAL TENSIONS AND THEN LEXINGTON AND CONCORD: APRIL 19, 1775

While the struggle with New York had been mainly about land, Ethan Allen had been increasingly linking the New York struggle with the overall tyranny of government, and he had been pleading his case to get sympathy in the *Connecticut (Hartford) Courant*:

> *The writs of Ejectment coming thick and faster. Women sobbing and lamenting, children crying and men pierc'd to the Heart with Sorrow and Indignation at the approaching Tyranny of New York.*

While John Brown was in Canada, unarmed farmers locked themselves in a courthouse in Westminster in the eastern part of the Grants to delay the session of the king's court scheduled for the next day. The county court officials were chosen by the New York legislature and were sympathetic to British policy rather than to the Continental Congress. On March 13, the farmers were fired upon, and two people died. Robert Cochran, from sixty miles away in Rupert, showed up within twenty-four hours with more than thirty Green Mountain Boys to help. Four hundred people overpowered the sheriff and his Tory sympathizers and then released the settlers. Tories, in turn, were arrested and taken to Northampton, Massachusetts, through Deerfield by Robert Cochran. Massachusetts and New Hampshire people had come to support the farmers. The land issue in the Grants was now more about the tyranny of government over the use of land and the tyranny of the British rules. One of the leaders of the citizens in this part was John Hazeltine, formerly of Salisbury, Connecticut, the early partner of Ethan Allen in the Salisbury blast furnace.

The tombstone of William French, who had been killed in the "Westminster Massacre," shows the shift—even in areas of the Grants that had been sympathetic to New York—to a feeling that the problems were King George III's fault. Part of French's tombstone reads:

Here William French his Body lies
For Murder his blood for vengance cries
King Georg the third his Tory crew
That with a bawl his head Shot threw
For Liberty and his Countrys Good
he Lost his Life his Dearest blood.

On April 18, 1775, three riders—Paul Revere, William Dawes and Dr. Samuel Prescott—began alerting the countryside that British troops were coming from Boston by sea to Concord (about twenty miles west) via Lexington to seize the powder and colonial supplies at Concord. The riders had a little help, since the British took two hours to travel from Boston because of a lack of boats. Ethan Allen will have similar issues later.

On the next day, April 19, 1775, although the British were able to destroy some of the supplies, the colonists fired upon the British at Concord and Lexington, hastening a retreat. There was now clearly open rebellion. Over the next week or so, colonists appeared from all over in Cambridge, which had become the headquarters of the resistance to the British, who were now in Boston. The siege of Boston had begun.

Part II
The Journey to Ticonderoga

JOURNEY STARTS IN HARTFORD, CONNECTICUT

About one week after the "shot heard 'round the world," Colonel Samuel H. Parsons of Connecticut left Cambridge and was returning to Hartford. On April 26, he met with a thirty-five-year-old captain from Connecticut's Second Regiment of Foot Guards on the way. The captain had about forty of his Foot Guards with him. He was Captain Benedict Arnold V (more commonly referred to as just Benedict Arnold).

Arnold was born in Norwich, Connecticut, to a well-to-do family but later moved to New Haven, where he made considerable money in trading and bookselling. Because of his trading and trips, he had occasion to go to the Lake Champlain area. He was also very upset at the British for their taxes, which affected his shipping business.

Colonel Parsons mentioned that there was a need for artillery and heavy cannons for the upcoming siege of Boston. Arnold mentioned that Fort Ticonderoga had a vast number of cannons. There is no record of either party suggesting the capture of Fort Ticonderoga. Arnold continued on to Cambridge with his foot guards. We will meet him later.

Parsons continued on to Hartford and arrived in the morning of April 27 (Thursday). Upon arrival, Parsons met with Samuel Wyllys and Silas Deane to discuss a venture to capture Fort Ticonderoga. Colonel Parsons also met with three other people: Thomas Mumford, Adam Babcock and Christopher Leffingwell.

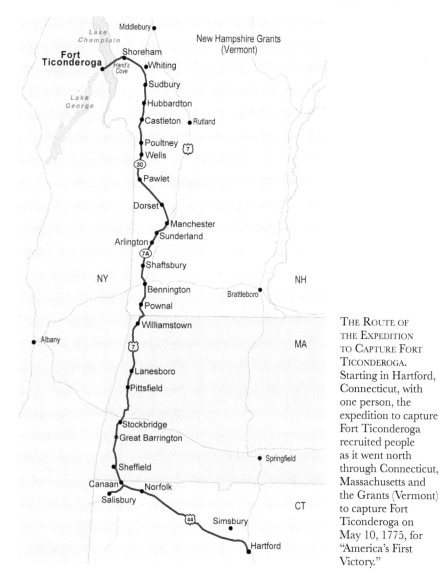

THE ROUTE OF THE EXPEDITION TO CAPTURE FORT TICONDEROGA. Starting in Hartford, Connecticut, with one person, the expedition to capture Fort Ticonderoga recruited people as it went north through Connecticut, Massachusetts and the Grants (Vermont) to capture Fort Ticonderoga on May 10, 1775, for "America's First Victory."

Although thousands of troops were being raised in Connecticut, this group decided that the best approach would be a surprise attack by a small, secret group with the help of the Green Mountain Boys. Many of the people settling the Grants were from Connecticut, and frequent articles in the *Connecticut Courant* on the plight of the settlers had created a sympathetic attitude. Connecticut was also not overly concerned about asking New York for permission to take a fort that was on its own soil.

The group making the decision was no lightweight. Leffingwell was a personal friend of Connecticut governor Jonathan Trumbull. Trumbull would be the only royally appointed governor to also serve as governor after the Revolution. By April 1775, Connecticut, under Trumbull, was basically operating as an colony independent from the Crown. Silas Deane was one of three Connecticut representatives to the First Continental Congress held the previous fall. Samuel H. Parsons had also been a classmate of Governor Trumbull's son.

This group began to procure men, provisions and money. The money came on April 28 from the state treasury as a "loan" with the personal guarantee of the individuals as shown on the two receipts:

Received of the Colony Treasury, One Hundred Pounds, to be applied to the Government's use, which we promise to account for to the satisfaction of the Colony.
April 28th, 1775

> *Christ Leffingwell*
> *Thos. Mumford*
> *Adam Babcock*
> *Sam H. Parsons*
> *Silas Deane*

Received of John Lawrence, Esq., Treasurer of the Colony of Connecticut, Two Hundred Pounds, lawful money. To be expended for the use of Government, and for which we promise to account to the satisfaction of the Colony.
April 28, 1775

> *Thos. Mumford*
> *Sam. H. Parsons*
> *Silas Deane*
> *Sam'l Wyllys.*

To put this £300 commitment into perspective, the governor of the colony of Connecticut received as a salary in 1775 the sum of £300.

The importance of supplying money cannot be overemphasized. This was not a government army, so everything, including travel expenses (food, horses, lodging and more), had to be purchased. Money also provided a degree of secrecy since it would give the cover that this expedition was perhaps nothing more than a hunting trip. On that same day, April 28, the money was given to Noah Phelps, an attorney from nearby Simsbury, and Bernard Romans, who immediately started off toward the Grants. Noah Phelps, who will play an important role as a spy later in the expedition, is buried in Simsbury.

On that same day, Edward Mott arrived in Hartford and met with Parsons, Deane and Leffingwell. They asked Mott if he would undertake the mission to Ticonderoga. As Elisha Phelps (who joined the group later) stated, "Our orders was to repair to the Grants of New Hampshire and raise an army of men." In the afternoon of the next day, April 29, Mott, who left Hartford with five people, spent the night at New Hartford and then, after getting a new horse in Norfolk, arrived Sunday, April 30 in Canaan, Connecticut, in the northwest corner—the upper lands. Being a small group, spread out and unarmed, they did not arouse suspicion from any local Tories who might warn Fort Ticonderoga. The path to Salisbury and Canaan is basically the Hartford-Albany route (now Route 44).

Salisbury and Canaan, Connecticut

On April 30, the group reached Canaan and the Lawrence House. (Captain Isaac Lawrence built it in 1751, and it still stands on Elm Street/Route 7.) Salisbury and Canaan were relatively free of Tories and full of friends of and connections to Ethan Allen. Although Ethan Allen had already moved to the Grants twelve years ago, his brother Heman still ran a store in Salisbury, and another brother, Levi, was a part-time Salisbury resident. The blast furnace he started was still operating. Thomas Young, who lived just across the border, had also moved on but had shown up the previous year in Boston as one of the disguised Sons of Liberty who poured tea into the harbor at the Boston Tea Party. Many of the towns in the Grants toward which the expedition was marching had settlers who had family and financial ties to Salisbury or were from Salisbury. Three future Vermont governors would be from Salisbury, including its first governor, Thomas Chittenden. Salisbury, Vermont, was also named after Salisbury, Connecticut.

One year after this group left Salisbury, on July 4, 1776, the Salisbury furnace operation that Ethan Allen had started would supply cannons for the Revolutionary War and would become known as the "Arsenal of the Revolution." Cannonballs and cannons up to thirty-two pounds were produced here. Connecticut itself would become the "Provision" colony of the Revolutionary War because of its huge supply of war matériel to the colonists.

The effort initiated by Samuel Parsons in Hartford grew one by one to sixteen people or more in the Connecticut group (see Appendix V). From Canaan itself, there was Captain John Stevens who joined the group; three of the "Salisbury volunteers" were Josiah Stoddard, Levi Allen and Samuel Blagden (who, as an aside, knew Benedict Arnold). Ashbel Wells had a "team" carry some baggage and other things. It is not clear if this was a carriage or some packhorses, but the Connecticut contingent had thought about the issue of provisions. Heman Allen, who had operated the store in Salisbury, would be sent ahead as an express to notify Ethan Allen that a group was coming to capture Fort Ticonderoga.

MASSACHUSETTS: SHEFFIELD TO WILLIAMSTOWN

Sheffield and Great Barrington

As the group moved north from the more established colony of Connecticut, it was more important to understand where people came from and their connection back to Connecticut rather than who they were at the time they were recruited. Crossing into Massachusetts, the group arrived on May 1 at Sheffield, about six miles north of Salisbury, where the group would also feel comfortable being among friends who had connections to Ethan Allen and Salisbury. Part of the group went to Mr. Dewey's place. Sheffield was the oldest town incorporated in western Massachusetts (1733), and one of the buildings in town, the Dan Raymond House, would have been there as the expedition went through. Ethan Allen's blast furnace partner Samuel Forbes lived here in the early 1740s, and Ethan Allen himself moved his family here in 1767 and was an occasional resident, although he spent most of his time exploring the Grants in the north country. However, he may have fathered two of his children here, Lucy Caroline and Mary Ann; his son, Joseph, may have died here. Ethan Allen had been here less than a month before in March. His younger brother by ten years, Zimri, would live here for ten years helping with the family farm.

From Sheffield, Jeremiah Halsey and Captain John Stevens (both of Connecticut) were sent to Albany to "ascertain the temper of the people." This was risky because if word got out to the royal governor, it could have stopped the entire mission. There is no clear indication that anyone from Sheffield at the time joined the group, as they were trying to keep their purpose a secret by staying small. However, two people from Sheffield who had moved previously to Shoreham (Amos Callender in 1774 and Elijah Kellog in 1766) would be recruited in the Grants. One of the Connecticut recruits, Ezra Hecock, joined the group in Sheffield. The group clearly must have stayed long enough in Sheffield to get information and possibly some supplies—they had contact with Ethan Allen's wife. Edward Mott's expense report for the trip included three pounds "to cash to Colonel Allen's wife." Since there were separate entries for expenses for the return trip, this three pounds to Allen's wife was most likely for the trip up.

Only three miles north of Sheffield was Great Barrington. In 1774, Great Barrington saw thousands involved in "the first open resistance to military rule imposed on Massachusetts in retaliation for the Boston Tea Party." With that kind of turnout, it was clear that the group could have recruited in Great Barrington easily. However, this risked secrecy, and their orders were to go to the Grants to raise men; a large body would have raised suspicions as they went north.

Stockbridge, Massachusetts

Spreading out, the small expedition made its way north from Great Barrington about six miles to Stockbridge, Massachusetts. On the road from Sheffield, Noah Phelps—who had left a day before the main group left Hartford and had apparently lingered in Connecticut—caught up with the group. Asa Eddy joined from Salisbury. The group arrived at Silas Bingham's place after 5:00 p.m. on Monday, May 1 on the way north. Silas Bingham's place was recognizable because it featured a red lion in the front; it still does today as the Red Lion Inn. Sometime about 1773 (the year of the Boston Tea Party), Silas Bingham and his wife, Anna, established a home that evolved into a general store and tavern.

Because of the nature of the stop, the expedition would not have drawn suspicion. The inn was at the crossroads of one of the east–west (Boston to Albany) roads and the north–south route up western Massachusetts. Therefore, as is today, the Red Lion Inn was used to hosting frequent travelers coming and going. Strong anti-English feeling prevailed in town. The first of several conventions in western Massachusetts to protest encroaching freedoms of the Intolerable Acts was held on July 6, 1774, at Silas Bingham's place. Even the Stockbridge Indians here supported the colonists' efforts; the Stockbridge Indians were the only tribe to serve in the Revolution. Accompanied by two lawyers and being from one of the older colonies, they might have looked more distinguished than normal travelers, as they had

RED LION INN, STOCKBRIDGE, MASSACHUSETTS. This photo was taken in 1866 and is one of the earliest surviving images of the Red Lion Inn. The expedition to capture Fort Ticonderoga stopped here on May 1, 1775. *Courtesy of the Red Lion Inn, Stockbridge, Massachusetts.*

money; they were merely harmless travelers, not an army, just going north. They weren't trying to recruit or even looking for anyone. Levi Allen joined later. To add to the ruse of just being travelers, Epaphras Bull bought some "Jack nives and Tobacco." The money from Connecticut had allowed the travelers to buy things as if on a surveying trip or hunting expedition. Many of the Connecticut patriots were unarmed, which also helped to stem any suspicion of the real intent of this group.

Pittsfield, Massachusetts

The expedition left Stockbridge, headed north about ten miles to Pittsfield and arrived late that same day, Monday, May 1. Levi Allen had joined them on the road. To avoid raising suspicion, the group was then disbursed somewhat, as some stayed at Mr. Root's and others stayed at Mr. Easterbrook's. Root was paid for the lodging provided so as to avoid suspicion. (This was also a period of extreme dislike for the Quartering Act, which demanded free lodging for military people.)

JAMES EASTON'S TAVERN SITE, PITTSFIELD, MASSACHUSETTS. Colonel Easton was a tavern owner and head of the local militia. The expedition to capture Fort Ticonderoga (with Easton as second in command) stopped here for key meetings.

The leader, Edward Mott, went to James Easton's tavern. There he met with Colonel James Easton and John Brown for a very strategic meeting. James Easton, born in Hartford in 1742, had gone to Litchfield, Connecticut. He was a regimental commander in the Massachusetts militia but also a deacon and tavern keeper. They also met "tall and powerful" John Brown (born 1744). His sister, Elizabeth, had married Oliver Arnold, attorney general of Rhode Island and a cousin of Benedict Arnold. This is the same John Brown who, after visiting Canada the month before with Peleg Sunderland, wrote to the Committee of Correspondence that Fort Ticonderoga should be taken if hostilities should break out and that the Green Mountain Boys were the ones who should do it. Brown appears to have been one of the Minutemen in the area but didn't have any rank on the upcoming expedition.

After Mott revealed their real purpose, Easton and Brown told the Connecticut group of the poverty and "scarcity of provisions" in the Grants and how "it would be difficult to raise a sufficient body of men there." They said that they should raise some extra troops in the Pittsfield area.

Easton offered to enlist men from his own regiment. As true patriots, both Easton and Brown offered to help and did not demand overall command of the expedition. Pittsfield had some of the most loyal patriots but also had, according to the minister, some of the worst Tories in the country.

To preserve secrecy, some of the group went on north to Bennington in the Grants the next day. After admitting Captain Israel Dickinson and some others to the group, Mott and Easton then split off and went over the mountain to Jericho (now Hancock), about four miles from Pittsfield, to see sixty-year-old Captain Asa Douglas of Easton's regiment to help recruit. Actually, the Douglas farm is located in what is now Stephentown, New York.

Asa Douglas played a big role in the capture of Fort Ticonderoga. Not only did he show deft recruiting skills (getting loyal people quickly), but he was also the one who successfully acquired boats so that the expedition could eventually cross Lake Champlain. (As a historical side note, one of Asa Douglas's descendants was Stephen A. Douglas, who was born in Brandon, Vermont, and was the Douglas of the famous Lincoln-Douglas debates in Illinois in the mid-1800s.)

Another person who was part of the Pittsfield Committee of Correspondence was another of Ethan Allen's cousins, Reverend Thomas Allen—later well known as "the Fighting Parson." He was against all forms of tyranny, including having concerns that the Continental Congress itself might go too far. His view was simple: he thought that Pittsfield should "remain in a state of nature," essentially with no government interference; such was also the nature of people involved with this expedition against British tyranny. He was part of the Pittsfield leadership group and sent a letter on May 4 that a post was on the way to Bennington to "hold his Green Mountain Boys in actual readiness."

Lanesboro and Williamstown, Massachusetts

Part of the group that didn't go to Jericho to recruit headed north (basically on today's Route 7/North Street in Pittsfield), arrived at eleven o'clock in the morning on Tuesday (May 2) in Lanesboro and stopped at Mr. Barnes's "just to rest horses."

Some of the group arrived in Williamstown (about fifteen miles from Pittsfield) about one o'clock in the afternoon on May 2, probably right at the site where the remnants of the former Fort West Hoosac were located (site of the current Williamstown Inn). From Lanesboro to Williamstown, they averaged about seven miles per hour. This group went on to Mr. Simons's in the north part of Williamstown and encountered twenty to thirty armed people who thought that this was a Tory contingent. The expedition made arrangements for provisions to be sent the following Saturday, May 7. Matthew Dunning—who was the son of a Baptist minister from south Williamstown—joined the group. At the next stop in the Grants, Pownal, Josiah Dunning will join the expedition.

Before leaving Massachusetts, the expedition recruited, in addition to the Connecticut contingent, maybe twenty-five from the Pittsfield area and then another fifteen (including Israel Harris and James Sargent) from Williamstown—bringing the total Massachusetts group to more than thirty-nine. Allowing for people who were recruited but didn't join that day or still had to gather things before they left, there were at least sixty who lived in Connecticut and Massachusetts at the time.

On to Bennington

On May 3, when part of the expedition entered Pownal (adjoining Williamstown) from Massachusetts, it crossed into another world, the Grants. Vermont in 1775 had about 12,000 people, whereas Massachusetts already had 235,000 people in 1770. It was the most recently settled colony (and most of that in last ten years), and there would be no cities in this unbroken wilderness. Hartford and Boston had been settled over one hundred years prior.

Although Pownal (named for a Massachusetts governor by Benning Wentworth) only had an estimated 350 people in 1775, it had at least 25 Green Mountain Boys. Although there were only 3 people identified from Pownal with Ethan Allen at Fort Ticonderoga, there is no record of any member of the expedition stopping to recruit. As before, the expedition probably wanted to get to Bennington as soon as possible and not arouse any suspicion. The expedition also knew that an express, Heman Allen, had been sent ahead and that Allen went to Bennington (the next town) so he could easily send back for the people he wanted. From Pownal was Josiah Dunning, who had enlisted with Captain Samuel Wright's company, and both were with Allen at Ticonderoga. Josiah Dunning, according to family records, may have been related to Matthew Dunning from Williamstown, the previous town. Since records mention Wright's company, some of these may be those unaccounted for. Additionally, the third person from Pownal

VERMONT SEGMENT OF THE EXPEDITION'S ROUTE TO FORT TICONDEROGA. As Ethan Allen recruited going north, he used the Castleton-Whiting portion of the original Onion River Land Company road and then parts of Crown Point Road to go west and arrive north of Fort Ticonderoga.

might be considered to be Captain Gideon Warren, who was also mentioned to from of Hampton, New York (just across the border), but was more associated with Pownal.

On the way to Bennington, at about six o'clock in the evening, John Brown and Levi Allen met "a man" who said that he had come directly from Fort Ticonderoga with news of "a reinforcement from Canada." Bull in his diary said that this "dampened our spirits." In fact these were the worst fears—that the British might know they were coming and that the British had definitely reinforced the fort. They decided to send someone back to Williamstown to stop the others from proceeding north until further orders. This same express evidently met Mott, who was behind the forward group. Mott questioned who this anonymous person was, got no clear answer and decided to press on to Bennington. What Mott didn't know was that there was some truth to what the man had said—Fort Ticonderoga had been reinforced recently.

Bennington

The main road that led from Pownal to Bennington (now Historic Route 7) passed the Jewett Tavern (built in 1770 and still there today as a private residence). Just past the tavern the road goes left and then immediately north up what is today Monument Avenue to what is today Old Bennington. Most of the troops reached Bennington on Wednesday, May 3.

Bennington only had about 585 people and ten to twelve buildings even fifteen years after it became the first town chartered under the New Hampshire Grants. The main Albany-Bennington-Brattleboro-Boston road crossed the main north–south road (now Monument Avenue) at the town green. Clustered around the green were Ethan Allen's home (currently the McCullough mausoleum is on the site) and, just to the north, the Catamount Tavern. In the middle of the green was the Old First Meetinghouse.

The Catamount Tavern (see image on page 23), with its "council room," had become the headquarters of the Green Mountain Boys, who for the last five years, from 1770 to 1775, had held off the claims of the government of New York. It was from here that Boys were dispatched all over Vermont—especially on the west side of the Green Mountains. It was here where Heman Allen had arrived with at least one day's notice that a group was coming from Connecticut and Massachusetts to ask for Allen's help to capture Fort Ticonderoga.

The leaders had to make a major decision, yes or no, on the capture of the fort. If the Green Mountain Boys attempted to capture Fort Ti and failed, surely the king would rule in favor of New York settlers in the land dispute issue. Even if the Boys captured Fort Ticonderoga, if the dispute that erupted at Lexington and Concord was settled, surely the king would refuse to recognize the existing New Hampshire titleholders. Furthermore, the fort itself was clearly located in New York, and they had no authority to capture it. What if they failed and were caught—there was the reward and

OLD BENNINGTON, VT

2.5 miles to Seth Warner Home Site (plaque)

⑧ Bennington Battle Monument ~306 ft. (elevator in season)

⑨ Seth Warner Monument

⑩ Bennington Battle Monument Gift Shop

WALLOOMSAC RD.

① Catamount Tavern Site (monument), Headquarters of Green Mountain Boys

② Ethan Allen Home Site (plaque) 1769-1775

③ Cemetery ~ Jonas Fay Grave (along fence)

④ Old First Church

⑤ First Meeting House Site (plaque)

⑥ Walloomsac Inn c1771 (private residence)

⑦ Nathaniel Brush House c1763 (private residence)

---- Original Road North to Fort Ticonderoga

BANK STREET

■ Samuel Robinson Home Site (plaque)

MONUMENT AVE.

① Catamount Tavern Site

② Ethan Allen Home Site

W. MAIN STREET

WEST RD.

9

2.0 miles to Samuel Herrick Home Site (plaque)

Scale

100 M
300 FT

■ Bennington Museum

■ Parson Dewey Home c1763 (private residence)

Right: ETHAN ALLEN'S BENNINGTON, VERMONT. Ethan Allen resided in this area (now Old Bennington) between 1769 and 1775. The key sites involved with 1775 have markers or are in existence today. Ethan Allen's minister's house, the Walloomsac Inn and the Nathaniel Brush House were all extant when Ethan Allen lived there and are private residences today.

Below: ETHAN ALLEN HOUSE MARKER, BENNINGTON, VERMONT. Ethan Allen lived in Bennington for six years prior to his march from Bennington to Fort Ticonderoga. The marker faces north on the southeast corner of the intersection of today's Route 9 and Monument Avenue. It is about fifty feet from where he lived and located across the street from the Catamount Tavern.

A FEW FEET SOUTH FROM THIS STONE STOOD THE HOUSE IN WHICH **ETHAN ALLEN** LIVED WHILE HE WAS A RESIDENT OF BENNINGTON 1769 — 1775

FIRST MEETINGHOUSE, BENNINGTON, VERMONT. Built in 1763–65, this is where Ethan Allen attended religious services and town meetings after the capture of Fort Ticonderoga in 1775. The current Old First Church nearby, "Vermont's Colonial Shrine," replaced it in 1806. A large tablet in the inscription marks the spot in the middle of the Old Bennington Green. *Courtesy Old First Church, Bennington Vermont.*

CATAMOUNT TAVERN MONUMENT, BENNINGTON, VERMONT. This marker on Monument Avenue is situated almost directly in front of where the Catamount Tavern's main door was located. It is also near the pole that had the stuffed catamount on it. Notice that the catamount is snarling toward the west, New York.

50

possible death waiting for many of the Green Mountain Boys, including Ethan Allen. What would Congress say if the king's fort was captured, since the Congress had protected the fort during the last session? Would this end all hope of a peaceful resolution of the Lexington and Concord events?

Was this a fool's mission? There were also the physical aspects of the fort. In some places it might have thirty-foot-high walls, and the Boys didn't have scaling equipment, nor had they ever attempted anything like this. Generally they didn't have bayonets and definitely did not have heavy artillery. Even if in disrepair, with just an hour's notice cannons could be placed strategically and with grapeshot kill twelve men in single blast, and the Boys only numbered maybe three hundred in total. How could they travel eighty miles recruiting and keep it a secret so that a Tory couldn't race to the fort with a warning. The British fort at Crown Point was only fifteen miles to the north, and reinforcements could be sent quickly from Canada. If the cannons were "spiked" so they couldn't be used by the colonists, nothing would be gained. With one hour's notice, the garrison at the fort could move guns into breaches in the wall—if there were any.

On the positive side, the group from Connecticut had money, so they could travel as a hunting party and not arouse suspicion. They could buy some provisions. The Connecticut group also had a quasi-legal status, since many of the people who signed the receipt were actually part of the Connecticut government. The Green Mountain Boys were organized, and they trusted Allen. They were masters of surprise, speed, secrecy and more. They were motivated. Tyranny of the church, tyranny of New York and tyranny of the British were all the same. They were willing to put personal interests and glory behind them.

Ethan Allen knew every nook and cranny of the landscape on the west side of Vermont (the Grants) as far north as Burlington—over forty miles north of Fort Ticonderoga. Allen may have also known everyone on the west side of Vermont. Any venture of this type would require knowing people—and not just superficially. If you ask someone to join, you better be sure that they might not reveal what you're going to do. This was very important in those days. The war had just broken out, and many people who were anti-New York were not anti-British and wanted to settle the dispute peaceably. Many of these people later became Tories. Others, who spoke of peace and reconciliation, became ardent revolutionaries. As of this time, no real offensive action had been taken against the king's property. All that was needed was one person who was not anti-British to warn the fort about the expedition coming, and it would be an almost impossible task to capture it.

Most importantly, Allen had the respect of the farmers and settlers. He almost single-handedly led the Green Mountain Boys for five years in successful monthly confrontations with New York and won. These were a variety of guerilla-type confrontations—quick, surprising, intimidating and well-organized attacks. He also seemed to have the knack for estimating the number of people needed. Sometimes only a few Boys were involved, but he never underestimated and had to send for reinforcements.

Ethan Allen would have none of this hesitation. In this critical debate, we have to rely on Allen's eloquent words. This idea of possibly reconciling the issues was, in effect, attempting "to explore futurity," but it was found to be "unfathomable." Ethan Allen summed up his views:

> *Ever since I arrived to a state of manhood, I have felt a sincere passion for liberty. The history of nations doomed to perpetual slavery, in consequence of yielding up to tyrants their natural born liberties, I read with a sort of philosophical horror; so the first systematical and bloody attempt at Lexington, to enslave America, thoroughly electrified my mind, and fully determined me to take part with my country.*

After all of the Connecticut and Massachusetts members arrived, there was held an informal or preliminary Council of War, established with James Easton as chairman. However, there was no question about whom the field leader would be. If Fort Ticonderoga was to be taken, it must be done quickly and as a surprise. Allen acted immediately, using the paramilitary skills he had acquired over the last five years. Allen sent Green Mountain Boys ahead to guard the roads to Fort Ticonderoga so that word of Lexington and Concord or their mission would not reach the fort. These guards were placed along the Fort Edward, Lake George, Skenesborough, Ticonderoga and Crown Point roads.

Some mustering of Green Mountain Boys had already been accomplished. The owner of the Catamount Tavern, Stephen Fay, had five sons, but one, Jonas, was a physician and had joined the group. Two years later, Jonas would draft the Vermont constitution, which was ratified in July 1777, when the Grants officially became Vermont. Fay would be paid for his services. Another Bennington local was Josiah Fuller, who apparently went along as a surgeon's mate.

Another key recruit was Samuel Herrick, who lived in the western part of Bennington about two miles away, and his homestead is marked today with a stone plaque. Another notable was Seth Warner, who also lived on the west side of town. Warner had come to Vermont from Roxbury, Connecticut (the northwest area), in 1763 and would live twenty years in the Grants before falling ill, returning to Roxbury and dying there. Warner may have come back from the north for this meeting. Warner would distinguish himself during the upcoming capture of the Fort Ticonderoga expedition, and two years later he would also be a hero at the Battle of Bennington.

Jeremiah Halsey and John Stevens returned from Albany at five o'clock at night and agreed with Mott that they should proceed, even after hearing about this other anonymous man telling them that the fort had been reinforced. They said that Albany had no problems, and they were even promised provisions. This had been risky, going into Albany and discussing the capture of the fort on New York's property. Then Captain Stevens and Gershom Hewitt went to Albany to purchase provisions and send them ahead. It was here in Bennington that Bernard Romans, originally from Europe, left the group. Mott, from Connecticut, commented that he "had been a trouble" anyway.

Before leaving Bennington on May 3, Noah Phelps and Ezra Hecock (or Heacock or Hickok) from Connecticut were sent to spy on the fort. Epaphras Bull from the Connecticut group gave Phelps a horse and commented, "And Capt Phelps should ride my horse." A rendezvous point was chosen so that they could recruit others and have them join later—Castleton, Vermont, about sixty miles to the north.

Part of the skill was to go north without being discovered by Tories. One way to disguise the intent of the group was to split the group, with some following behind the others on the same road. The other way was to occasionally take a separate side route, if available. Since the groups did not have artillery, uniforms, bayonets or even tents, they could pass for a hunting expedition or as surveyors inspecting land to the north.

Recruiting would have to be done one by one and personally over a vast, sparsely populated area with remote farms. Recruiters couldn't waste time. They would have to go directly to remote farms to handpick known loyal people. There was no other way to recruit, since there were no forts or even armories between Bennington and Fort Ticonderoga (about ninety miles away) to which Ethan Allen could go and acquire a couple of hundred soldiers at once. There were also those Green Mountain Boys who were anti–New York in the land issue but not necessarily anti-British on the government issue, as it would turn out.

Some members of the expedition left the Catamount Tavern on Friday, May 5 at 9:00 a.m. to march north to Castleton. They went up Monument

BENNINGTON BATTLE MONUMENT, BENNINGTON, VERMONT. Looking north up Monument Avenue from the Catamount Tavern, at more than 306 feet tall the monument stands where the original road running to Fort Ticonderoga was located. In 1911, Olin Scott had the statue of Seth Warner, third in command at the capture of Fort Ticonderoga, erected in the foreground. The monument today is administered by the State of Vermont.

Avenue (where the 306-foot-tall Bennington Battle Monument is today), down the hill and then up Harwood Hill. Hugging the foothills to avoid the swamps, they then followed up the Vermont Valley along what is today the Historic 7A corridor between the Green Mountains to the east and the Taconic range to the west.

BENNINGTON TO MANCHESTER

In Shaftsbury, about six miles north of Bennington, the road passes a stone house built in 1769 and later owned by Robert Frost (now a museum). Farther north, the group arrived at 10:30 a.m. at the Galusha Tavern, where there were plenty of connections and loyal friends to recruit. They had been traveling about four miles per hour. Inns during the colonial period were normally small and started out as homes. Converting to an inn or at least

DAVID GALUSHA TAVERN, SHAFTSBURY, VERMONT. Some members of the expedition north stopped at David Galusha's tavern. The inn/tavern was built about 1775. The original structure could have been built over a period of time. David Galusha was a Green Mountain Boy in Seth Warner's regiment. The house is now a private residence.

offering lodging services was a quick way to get cash. The Galushas were friends with Seth Warner and the Allens. David Galusha (born 1748) was the brother of Jonas Galusha (born 1753), later seven-time governor of Vermont from Salisbury, Connecticut.

Jonas Galusha had married Mary Chittenden from Salisbury, the daughter of Thomas Chittenden, the first governor of Vermont and who was also from Salisbury, Connecticut. Another daughter of Thomas Chittenden married Matthew Lyon, who had moved to Wallingford, Vermont, in 1774 from Woodbury—Seth Warner's and Remember Baker's town. This was a good place to recruit. Lyon headed a company of Green Mountain Boys and would be with Allen at the capture of Fort Ticonderoga. Another 1769 house is just up the road just before the 1790 house built by Jonas Galusha.

Six miles to the north after Shaftsbury was Arlington, with only 320 people, which posed a major problem for the group heading to capture Fort Ticonderoga. Different religious sects had settled various towns in Vermont. Arlington was settled primarily by Episcopalians, who at the time were almost identical to those from the Church of England. Hence, there were many Tory sympathizers in Arlington. In fact, there were so many sympathizers that Arlington was also referred to as "Tory Hollow." Some Arlington homes today have National Register statuses as hiding places for Tories. Although Remember Baker, a fervent Green Mountain Boy, had built a gristmill in Arlington maybe ten years before and was with Allen at Ticonderoga, he was up north in Burlington at the time.

In his diary, Epaphras Bull from Connecticut makes reference to stopping at "Holly's," where he "borrowed a gun." It seems pretty remarkable to

HAWLEY-CROFUT HOUSE/TAVERN, ARLINGTON, VERMONT. This house also served as a tavern and was built in 1773 by or for Abel Hawley. The expedition stopped here on the road to capture Fort Ticonderoga. It is now a private residence.

come one hundred miles to capture a fort and then have to borrow a gun. Also, what was the guy thinking when he "lent" Bull a gun to capture a fort? A study of land records and other sources reveals no Holly in Arlington. However, west on what is now Route 313—then about one hundred yards west of Tory Lane—there was the "Hawley House" (more recently referred to as the Crofut-Hawley House and still extant). Abel Hawley lived in the house, which was also built as a tavern. As the Revolution went on, this tavern served both Green Mountain Boys and Tories. Abel Hawley himself eventually sided with Britain. Bull must have meant Hawley instead of Holly. Even further evidence of this is that Bull refers to the town of "Pollet," or Pawlet, so perhaps substituting "aw" for "ol" was Bull's way of speaking or writing, and so "Holly's" becomes "Hawley's."

The expedition, now with more than sixty people, was somehow able go through a town full of Tory sympathizers, borrow a gun and still avoid having a Tory taking off to warn Ticonderoga. It is very possible that the group split up, with some of the group going up over what is today Tory Lane to pick up Historic 7A again.

The routes north from Arlington cut through the northwest corner of Sunderland. Some members of the group passed here at 2:00 p.m. without stopping. One of the captains of the Green Mountain Boys, Gideon Warren, apparently had ties here (he was also with Allen at Fort Ticonderoga). There is no indication of where he actually picked up the expedition. Because Ethan Allen traveled frequently, he certainly may have stayed in Sunderland previously. Ethan and his brother Ira eventually lived in Sunderland, but much later, and built a house (now the Ira Allen House on Historic 7A). The document on which Thomas Young and Ethan Allen worked in Salisbury,

Connecticut, would become Ethan Allen's manifesto in a sense, "Reason: The Only Oracle of Man." Ethan Allen would supposedly present the first copy to his wife, Fanny, many years later at the Ira Allen House.

Although the expedition was spreading out to avoid detection, it made its way up the Historic 7A corridor (the original road was located a little to the west, starting at Lathrop Lane) into Manchester and arriving at four o'clock in the afternoon. It appears that over 50 members of the expedition were in Manchester at one time. Manchester, with about 340 people, had a smaller population than Bennington in the south, although it was about the same size as Arlington at 320.

Unlike many other towns in the Grants, Manchester had been settled by people from New York—Amenia, actually, which is just over the New York line near Connecticut. (Amenia had been the home of Ethan Allen's mentor, Thomas Young.) Manchester had become a more open town. In fact, the taverns in Manchester were built before the churches. Given the size of the group and the number of taverns, it was logical that they would stop here, because they could split up among many eating places and not be conspicuous. Since the group from Connecticut had money, it would have been easy to purchase food and not raise suspicions.

INN AT ORMSBY HILL, MANCHESTER, VERMONT. This inn was built in 1770, or even as early as 1764, and is on the road to Fort Ticonderoga. It was built by Thompson Purdy. Peleg Sunderland, who was with Ethan Allen at Ticonderoga, married into the Purdy family.

ELIAKIN WELLER TAVERN, MANCHESTER, VERMONT. Built in 1774, the Green Mountain Boys met here, and in March 1774 a convention held here supported the Green Mountain Boys against New York land claimants. Weller's daughter married Benjamin Roberts, one of the six Robertses (father and five sons) who were with Allen at the capture of Fort Ticonderoga. It is now a private residence.

In their own words, the citizen-soldiers on this journey "dined" in Manchester. Located about one mile before reaching Manchester Village was the Purdy House on Historic 7A, which is now the Inn at Ormsby Hill. Christopher Roberts married into the Purdy family and by this marriage became a brother-in-law of Peleg Sunderland (the man who accompanied John Brown to Canada the previous month to assess the situation there). The Purdy home was therefore known to the group moving north and was a good starting place to recruit fervent Green Mountain Boys. Both Christopher Roberts and Peleg Sunderland were with Ethan Allen at the capture of Fort Ticonderoga.

Just past the Purdy place was the Weller Tavern. The sympathies of the Wellers were well known, and during the previous year, 1774, a convention was held at the Weller Tavern for Green Mountain Boys, who passed a resolution forbidding any Grants people from holding office in the king's province of New York. Eliakin Weller's daughter, Annice, married Benjamin Roberts, the son of John Roberts. Benjamin Roberts, along with his five brothers and his father, joined the expedition to Fort Ticonderoga (two of his sons lived in Dorset, the next town north). They became known as the "Fighting Roberts." Between these two inns, members of the expedition could recruit the largest immediate family and others to be with Ethan Allen at Fort Ticonderoga. Both John Roberts (the father) and Christopher Roberts are buried at the Dellwood Cemetery, fifty yards south of the Weller Tavern. Stephen Smith and Peleg Sunderland, both of Manchester, also joined the expedition to Fort Ticonderoga.

A little farther up the hill in Manchester (now referred to as Manchester Village) was another potential place to dine and recruit, the Marsh Tavern. Built in 1769, it was located at the present southern wing of the Equinox

The Journey to Ticonderoga

GRAVES OF JOHN AND CHRISTOPHER ROBERTS, DELLWOOD CEMETERY, MANCHESTER, VERMONT. The small Daughters of the American Revolution (DAR) marker near the grave to the right is for John Roberts, and the other DAR marker on the grave to the left is for his son, Christopher Roberts. The six Robertses (father and five sons) composed the largest immediate family on the expedition that captured Fort Ticonderoga.

Resort and Spa; this is the basis of the Equinox claiming to have been "established [in] 1769." At the time, the very loyal patriot Martin Powell managed it. Eating at Marsh's tavern would have had its risks since the tavern owner, William Marsh, would later show his true feelings by fleeing to Canada as a Tory. He did return after the war and is buried at the nearby East Dorset cemetery. Another risk concerning the Marsh Tavern was that Marsh's father-in-law, Jeremiah French, owned the house diagonally across the street. Although built in the early 1770s, the house is now known as the "1811 House." French, who also became a Tory, was the largest landowner in Manchester and owned almost all of the land on the east side of the road. French actually joined the British forces; he was captured and later died in Canada. The expedition somehow was able to get through Manchester without any current or potential Tories getting the word to Fort Ticonderoga.

Nestled in the Vermont Valley between the Taconic Mountains to the west, with their 3,800-foot-tall Mount Equinox, and the Green Mountains to the

MARSH TAVERN • 1769
MANCHESTER, VERMONT

Manchester Historical Society

MARSH TAVERN, MANCHESTER, VERMONT. The Green Mountain Boys met here. The tavern was located where the south wing of the Equinox Resort and Spa is located today. William Marsh later became a Tory. *Courtesy Manchester Historical Society and William Badger.*

EQUINOX RESORT AND SPA, MANCHESTER, VERMONT. The roots of the hotel go back to 1769 with the Marsh Tavern. The foundation of the Marsh Tavern is located on the southernmost wing of the current hotel (to the left).

east, Manchester represented a logistical issue. From the Marsh Tavern, the expedition could get to the rendezvous at Castleton through the Vermont Valley (basically using West Road and then Morse Hill Road to Route 7) to Rutland, with its larger population, and finally west to Castleton. Another, shorter option was to cut through the break in the Taconic range by going down Manchester West Road (the actual road was located more to the west, where Three Maple is today) and out through Dorset West Road and then north on the Route 30 corridor directly into Castleton. Going north up the Vermont Valley via Historic Route 7A would have required passing the William Marsh farm in East Dorset.

The expedition chose to go out through the Taconics and up the Route 30 corridor to Castleton. After an hour and half stop for dinner and recruiting in Manchester, three of the group left at 5:30 p.m. on Friday, May 5 to head out Manchester West Road toward Dorset. The remaining party stayed in Manchester. This is very revealing of the tactics used to thin out the group to avoid detection or suspicion.

FROM DORSET TO THE CASTLETON RENDEZVOUS

The expedition then took Dorset West Road because that portion of Route 30 at the time had wetlands. The Dorset West Road was well traveled, as indicated by the presence of the Cephas Kent Inn (circa 1775 and still there today) at the junction of Nichols Hill Road and Dorset West Road. It is about six miles from the Marsh Tavern. Cephas Kent was an ardent fighter against the king's New York province policies and land interests. (Tyler Resch, in his very thorough book *Dorset in the Shadow of Marble Mountain*, details the subtle differences between the Cephas Kent Tavern and the Kent Inn—both located at the same intersection.)

Across the road to the east of the Kent Inn is "Kent Meadows" where, according to tradition, the Green Mountain Boys camped on their way to Fort Ticonderoga. Additionally, just south of the meadows and about thirty feet off Dorset West Road is the Ethan Allen Spring, listed as a Vermont historic site. It seems logical that Kent Meadows, being flat and having a tavern and water, would be a good camping (staging) area; some people went ahead. There are also roads running east from Dorset to areas like Danby, to which Ethan Allen could have ridden to recruit. Taking Dorset West Road north and up Foote Road for a short stretch and then back to Dorset West Road, the expedition crossed into Rupert.

KENT MEADOWS, DORSET, VERMONT. Looking east, Ethan Allen and the members of the expedition to Fort Ticonderoga were said to have camped here. The stone marker on the far left (just the edge is visible) is in front of the still-standing Cephas Kent Inn built circa 1775. Several hundred yards to the south (to the right, off the picture) is the Ethan Allen Spring, which is listed on the State of Vermont register of historic sites.

Shocking News at Rupert

Rupert also gives some insight into how the expedition was able to travel without being discovered. Three members had come to Rupert but had left a larger group of about fifty behind in Manchester to acquire some provisions. Then, when the others came up, some stayed in Rupert while the others went ahead. Most of the early settlement of Rupert took place in the western part near Indian River and not in east and north Rupert (the Mettowee Valley), where the old Indian trail, now Route 30, goes north.

The first contingent reached Rupert in the evening of May 5 after traveling from Bennington since 9:00 a.m. Some spent the night in Rupert at Mr. Smith's. Including stops, they had averaged about three miles per hour for thirty miles from Bennington. Although Rupert only had 230 people in 1775, the town contributed one the most fervent Green Mountain Boys, Robert Cochran, to the expedition. This is the same Robert Cochran who was a captain in the Green Mountain Boys company and was on the wanted-for-death list from New York. One month earlier, Cochran led over 30 Green

Mountain Boys to Westminster, Vermont, sixty miles away, to help the settlers involved in the Westminster Massacre. Cochran had moved to Bennington in 1768 and then moved to Rupert. Luke Noble, who was probably about fifteen at the time, joined the expedition. He is now buried in Rupert.

Although small, the expedition had to be careful because Rupert did have several Tory-leaning residents who might have warned Ticonderoga. In fact, a Tory stole many of the town records from that period.

More difficult to deal with than possible Tories were several "very authentic" reports received in Rupert by Ethan Allen and the expedition: Fort Ticonderoga had been reinforced, and there were eighty men at Ticonderoga, plus "they are repairing the fort." However, as Bull states in his diary, the group was "resolute and want to proceed." This would be the worst news in two ways. Even if there were only a few people garrisoned in the fort, they would have had time—as the attack would not be scheduled for five days—to prepare by putting grapeshot in the cannons and moving them to any wall breaches. They could also "spike" the guns to render them useless to the colonists in case they felt outnumbered. Even worse, if they knew ahead of time, they could get reinforcements from Canada or His Majesty's Fort at Crown Point, only fifteen miles away north on Lake Champlain.

This didn't bother Allen or the group. The contingent decided to press on. What they didn't know was that the fort had actually been recently reinforced from Canada.

Pawlet-Wells-Poultney

Some members of the group would spend the next night in Rupert, and some would leave that day, Saturday, May 6, to head north to Castleton. The next town was Pawlet, and with four hundred residents it was bigger than Manchester. The intersection of the current Routes 30 and 149 is known today as Blossom's Corner. Timothy Allen—who had come from Woodbury, Connecticut, in 1768—was a cousin of Ethan Allen's. This area became the homestead of David G. Blossom, hence Blossom's Corner. The Mettewee River is located near here, and the area is flat, leading to accounts that some of the Green Mountain Boys camped here on the way to Fort Ticonderoga. The expedition knew the area well because of Timothy Allen. Remember Baker was actually a proprietor of Pawlet and a "temporary resident" as early as 1768. Dr. Jonas Fay from Bennington—who was with the expedition as surgeon—also lived here after the capture.

A few members of the expedition went through Wells on Sunday, May 7, but there was no clear indication that any stopped here. However, the Green Mountain Boys liked to hunt in Wells, so they certainly knew the roads.

Some members of the group said that they "refreshed ourselves and horses" in the very friendly town of Poultney with its 230 people. All but one person apparently supported the Revolution, so a Tory sending a warning to Ticonderoga was remote here. It was from Poultney that the reward for the New York attorney general was posted, generating loyalty to Ethan Allen among local settlers. In the early 1770s, over one-third of the land in Poultney was owned by the Allen family. In the first town meeting on March 8, 1775 (two months before the capture of Fort Ticonderoga), Heber Allen had been elected as first town clerk. Ethan Allen had been elected the town's proprietors clerk in 1772. In fact, Ethan Allen's first land purchases took place here in Poultney and in the next town to the north, Castleton.

The first two settlers of Poultney were Thomas Ashley and Ebenezer Allen, a cousin of Ethan Allen's. Needless to say, both of these individuals joined the expedition to capture Fort Ticonderoga. Heber Allen is buried in Poultney. It will be Ebenezer Allen who moves to South Hero Island, north of Burlington, and with whom Ethan Allen will be visiting when he dies fourteen years later in 1789.

RENDEZVOUS AT CASTLETON: EXTENSIVE PREPARATIONS

Notwithstanding that it would be hard not to raise suspicion in Castleton, with over 170 people camping in a town in which only 175 residents lived at the time, Allen had chosen the perfect town for a rendezvous. It was near Fort Ticonderoga but not so close that it would arouse suspicion from the fort itself. Allen owned land there and was familiar with the people in town. The road Ira Allen and Remember Baker built could be used to head north, pick up the Crown Point Road and then go west to Fort Ticonderoga and arrive in secrecy north of the fort. Allen had friends in nearby towns—including Rutland, with a larger population at about 615—who could provide recruits.

The two settlers who built the first permanent home six years prior in Castleton were Amos Bird and Noah Lee of Salisbury, Connecticut. Bird sold some of his land to Zadock Remington to build a tavern. (Noah Lee would join the expedition to Fort Ticonderoga, as would Nehemiah Hoit, a deacon. George Foote of Castleton would also join.) Down the road from

RENDEZVOUS POINT, CASTLETON, VERMONT. A marker in front of the Federated Church of Castleton marks the location of Richard Bentley's farm and house, where the Committee of War met.

the inn, in front of the current Federated Church, was the farm and house of Richard Bentley.

As the expedition from Connecticut and the south started to arrive in the evening of Sunday, May 7, some of the men and officers were stationed at Remington's Tavern. The Council of War met at Bentley's farmhouse. A Remington Tavern rendering indicates two stories, two chimneys—each about one-third from each end—five windows on the second floor and four on the first and a door. The middle window on the second floor is decorative and there are small side windows on the door and center window. Three windows are shown on the second floor at the end over three windows on the end of the ground floor.

Although Castleton mainly had rebels in town and didn't seem to be a problem to Allen, the irony is that Zadock Remington had been accused of Tory leanings, and his brother, David, became a prominent Tory.

On Monday, May 8, there was a vote on how to proceed. Voting was the essence of why these people were on this mission. The Crown had basically closed down Massachusetts, allowing no say from the legislature.

In Connecticut and elsewhere there was "taxation without representation," and in Vermont the king and the king's royal governor (New York) were interfering with the courts and land titles without local participation.

Although there had been some form of a Council of War in Bennington, there was now a more formal council. The following command structure was voted:

- Edward Mott, Connecticut, Chairman of the Committee of War
- Ethan Allen, New Hampshire Grants (Vermont) Field Commander
- James Easton, Massachusetts, Second in Command
- Seth Warner, New Hampshire Grants (Vermont) Third in Command

As was custom, the structure for commanders was based on the number of people recruited.

Another order of business was the issue of boats for crossing Lake Champlain. Noah Lee (one of the first settlers and formerly of Salisbury) suggested Skene's boats in Skenesborough, located at the southern tip of Lake Champlain. It was then agreed that Samuel Herrick was to go in the afternoon the next day, May 9, to capture Major Skene's boats. Major Skene was the son of a wealthy merchant and landowner who controlled the area at the southern portion of Lake Champlain. This almost herculean task would require thirty people to travel fifteen miles from Castleton to Skenesborough and then go north twenty miles past Fort Ticonderoga to the final jumping-off place, Hand's Cove on Lake Champlain.

As Allen had learned through his fight with New York, backup plans are advised. He therefore sent Captain Asa Douglas from Hancock (Jericho), Massachusetts, who had recruited Massachusetts troops with James Easton the previous week, north toward Panton and Crown Point to see if some boats could be acquired. Apparently, there was the thought of going across the lake to "hire" some of the king's boats at the British fort at Crown Point, which apparently had been done before for fishing or other activities. Another account has him going north to seek advice from a relative who lived in that area.

Beach's Sixty-Mile Twenty-Four-Hour Trip

Another order of business was getting more men. To this end, Ethan Allen sent a messenger, Samuel Beach (1752–1829), to recruit Green Mountain Boys and have them meet at Hand's Cove (Herrick's Cove at the time) in

The Journey to Ticonderoga

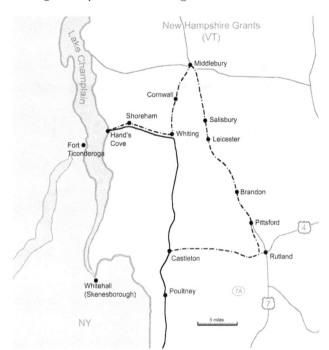

Shoreham on the eastern shore of Lake Champlain. At the time, Major Samuel Beach's father, Gershom, lived in the Rutland area.

This recruiting ride of more than sixty miles in about twenty-four hours would rival the Lexington and Concord warning rides of William Dawes, Paul Revere and Dr. Prescott. One report had Beach on foot, but that may be interpretation of the word "tramped." He had to know exactly whom he could trust and where their remote cabins would be located over this vast, lightly settled countryside and, as they had done for the last five years, ensure commitments to leave immediately. It also represents the apex of loyalty to Ethan Allen. The settlers didn't have to understand what the purpose was—all they knew was that Allen had protected their land rights for five years; if they heard "Allen needs you at Ti," they would drop everything and go.

Major Beach's (he wasn't made a major until after the war) first stop would be Rutland (named Socioborough under a New York patent issued in 1771 in violation of the British order of 1767). Many details of Beach's trip are not known (understandable since he was a blacksmith and in no hurry to document everything), but he probably went to the tavern house of a fervent patriot and friend of the Green Mountain Boy, James Mead. Mead was first permanent Rutland settler in 1771 and was a "judge" in the recent

"ALLEN NEEDS YOU AT TI." One of several recruiters, Major Beach is portrayed here recruiting Green Mountain Boys. That is all the recruiters had to say—there was complete trust in Ethan Allen. The clothes are typical, and the gun, without bayonet, was the type used at the capture of Fort Ticonderoga. The illustration also depicts the urgency. *Reprinted by permission of National Life Group. Artwork by Herbert M. Stoops. First published in the* Saturday Evening Post and Time, *1947.*

trial in nearby Tinmouth of a "Yorker." Mead's Tavern was located in what is today Center Rutland on West Proctor Road, just west of the Otter Creek and main downtown Rutland. (The Tavern is marked today with a tablet.) Mead provided information about routes and who else might be available to go. His tavern was located on a section of the Crown Point Road.

From Mead's Tavern, the Crown Point Road runs about seven miles north to Pittsford, a town of 160 people in 1775. Pittsford was one of the towns in the Otter Creek Valley. Beach knew who to contact. Captain Benjamin Cooley (1747–1810) was Beach's brother-in-law, since he had married Beach's sister, Ruth (born 1758), in 1773. Cooley got his gun and recruited four others: Isaac Buck Jr., John Deming, Hopkins Rowley and Ephraim Stevens. Beach then went on to Brandon, with only about eighty recruits, and then on to Leicester, which had only been settled in 1773.

Next after Leicester in this wilderness was Salisbury. The first proprietors meeting in 1762 had taken place in Salisbury, Connecticut, at the John Evarts (or Everts) Tavern—still there as a private home. As late as December 1774, the proprietors meetings were held in Salisbury, Connecticut. Samuel Keep, who was with Allen at Fort Ti, was from Salisbury and was one of original grantees of Salisbury, Vermont, but he came there after the war from Crown

Point, New York, where he had settled in 1773. One unconfirmed story has Keep, on the pretense of looking for a cow, gaining access to the grounds and making a survey of the fort in preparation of the attack. No surprise that Keep went to Salisbury, Vermont, and "immediately" engaged in the business of iron making, because like Salisbury, Connecticut, there were iron ore deposits. Of course, Vermonters know that Salisbury is home to Ann Story, who survived the rugged wilderness in Revolutionary War times and inspired the Ann Story Chapter of the Daughters of the American Revolution (DAR).

Beach's next stop of Middlebury, eight miles north of Salisbury, was another town with connections to Salisbury, Connecticut, and to Ethan Allen. On November 2, 1761, Middlebury was chartered, and on the next day Salisbury, Vermont, was chartered. Both towns had grantees from Salisbury, Connecticut. One of the other proprietors was Thomas Chittenden, Vermont's first governor and also from Salisbury, Connecticut. Although the first actual settlements in Middlebury were as recent as 1773, Middlebury's Colonel John Chipman—who was born in 1744 in Salisbury, Connecticut—would join the expedition. (John Chipman's cousins would also distinguish themselves in Vermont.)

Moving south, Beach went through Cornwall, which was named after Cornwall, Connecticut, where Ethan Allen's family was from early on. The first proprietors meetings were held in Salisbury, Connecticut. Although Cornwall had many ties to Allen and was a natural place to recruit, there is no one indentified by name from Cornwall with the expedition to capture Fort Ticonderoga. Perhaps its small size limited available recruits.

SAMUEL BEACH GRAVE SITE, WHITING, VERMONT. The large tombstone, silhouetted by today's Whiting Community Church in the background, is that of Major Samuel Beach.

Whiting, the next town going south and located about four miles from Cornwall, had been chartered in 1763, the first settlers only starting to arrive about 1775. The first proprietors were mainly from Massachusetts. Beach himself did not live in Whiting at the time, nor was it heavily populated, so he probably did not spend much time in Whiting in May 1775. Mainly due to this recruiting run, the government awarded him land in Whiting (as it turns out, on the Crown Point Road west of town). Land records show that he closed on May 12, 1786, which would have made him about thirty-four. He actually became the surveyor and first town representative of Whiting and received his commission as major after the war. Unfortunately, he apparently died poor and in debtors' prison.

The marker in front of the current Whiting Community Church reads:

Major Samuel Beach
1752–1829
"The Paul Revere of Vermont"
He lies buried in this cemetery. He walked 64 miles to recruit men to aid
Ethan Allen in the Capture of Fort Ticonderoga, May 10, 1775

Erected by the Vermont Chapter National Society Daughters of Founders
and Patriots of America 1956.

Both Samuel Beach and his father Gershom were with Allen at Ticonderoga. As Beach could not have stopped for long, some of the residents in each town may have come in after he left and been part of the gathering of men in Hand's Cove. The recruiting run ended in Shoreham. This small town—with only six families residing here before 1775 and a total estimated population of about thirty in 1775—provided at least seven for the expedition. Goodhue states that "nine" men from Shoreham who lived in town either before or after the capture are known to have been with Allen when he entered the fort: Nathan Beman, Amos Callender, John Crigo, Elijah Kellog, Thomas Rowley Jr., Samuel Wolcott and Samuel Wolcott Jr. plus Hopkins Rowley (mostly associated with Pittsford) and Stephen Smith (mostly associated with Manchester). If Hopkins Rowley and Stephen Smith are deducted from Goodhue's list, that leaves seven. However, after Goodhue's book, Robert O. Bascom listed four more from Shoreham who were with Allen upon entering the fort: Noah Callender, Noah Jones, Daniel Newton and Nathan Smith Jr., which would give a total of eleven from Shoreham. Goodhue mentions the latter but perhaps was not sure if they actually entered the fort with Allen. Bascom indicates that they did, so the total would be eleven. Also, it should be remembered that Elijah Kellog and Amos Callender were from Sheffield, Massachusetts, which was on the route to Ticonderoga. In his recruiting run, Beach had gone through Pittsford. In any event, for this small of a town, this is a remarkable number of people.

The Spy Mission Returns

While Beach was on his twenty-four-hour recruiting run, back in Castleton Noah Phelps returned "Tuesday morning may 9" from his spy mission. He had left Bennington to go north to the lake. Noah Phelps (1740–1809), a lawyer from Simsbury, Connecticut, may have been America's first true spy, and he was a good one. Before Lexington and Concord and during the land disputes, Allen had practice using spies since he had sent his brother into Albany to get some facts on rumored British troops moving up the Hudson River. Some accounts have Phelps staying overnight and hearing British soldiers in the next room talking about the condition of Fort Ticonderoga. Pretending to need a shave, Phelps gained entrance into the fort. Although some accounts have him "disguising" himself as a woodsman, he was probably given the outfit of the day and had to just pretend to be a woodsman. This is a tribute to Noah Phelps, a Yale graduate and attorney, who was willing to risk his life with this dangerous venture.

Phelps was actually able to meet the commander, Captain Delaplace. In addition to observing some breaches in the fort walls, tradition notes that on the way out Phelps heard the commander indicate that they were having a problem with wet powder. (One account has Phelps saying that the commander said "all.") Phelps had to avoid using certain mannerisms that would give him away, although it seems that some of the British were getting suspicious.

As the story goes, Phelps left by boat with someone rowing and then crossed the lake to get to Castleton on May 9. One story has him brazenly employing a boatman from the fort to row him across the lake, protesting that he was not an oarsman. When out of range of the fort, the oarsman became suspicious when Phelps took an oar and started rowing vigorously. Phelps hurried to Castleton to report what he had seen and heard. Noah Phelps is buried in Simsbury, and his brother, Elisha, was also with him on the expedition to capture Fort Ticonderoga.

A THUNDERBOLT: BENEDICT ARNOLD APPEARS

Allen had left Castleton by Monday, May 8 to head to the lake to meet some people at Wessels, which is a house/tavern just north of Castleton about fifteen miles in Sudbury. It shows up on British maps as one of the only buildings in the area near the Otter Creek and was in existence as early as 1759.

Although provided good news about the condition of the fort, Allen needed more specific information about the fort beyond what Noah Phelps had supplied. Allen, who had stayed with some of the local Shoreham settlers, went to a farmer who said that he wasn't familiar with the fort but that his teenage son, Nathan, had played in the fort over the years and knew the layout exactly. The expedition had a guide. It also had another future family connection, since Nathan Beman (who was originally from Manchester) married Jemina Roberts, a daughter of John Roberts, who was there from Manchester with his five sons. Nathan Beman would eventually go to upstate New York with Benjamin Roberts, who had married Annice Weller, the daughter of the Manchester tavern owner. Nathan Beman would be one of the original founders of Chateaugay, New York.

But after Allen left, a thunderbolt struck in the form of trouble. Benedict Arnold appeared at four o'clock in the afternoon on Monday, May 8 in a brilliant formal uniform and accompanied by one other person, a wardrobe assistant. Those at Castleton were pleased to see this man in a bright Connecticut Foot Guard uniform but were shocked when he demanded to become the commander of the expedition! The basis of his claim was a commission that he carried from the Massachusetts Committee of Safety.

Arnold's claim goes back three weeks, to his April 26 meeting with Samuel Parsons outside of Hartford. Just after Lexington and Concord, Benedict Arnold had rallied about forty of his local Connecticut Foot Guards and

BENEDICT ARNOLD'S HOUSE, NEW HAVEN, CONNECTICUT. Benedict Arnold was a well-to-do merchant, and this house (at 155 Water Street) at the time was located on the waterfront. In the 1960s, redevelopment filled in major parts of the port. *Courtesy Connecticut Historical Society.*

then threatened to break into the local supply depot in New Haven where he lived if the local leaders wouldn't give him the key to the powder and arms so that he could go to Cambridge and help the colonists. The committee relented and gave him the key. On the road to Cambridge he met Parsons, who was going to Hartford and eventually started the wheels in motion that would produce the expedition that was now in Castleton.

Arnold, however, went in the opposite direction, continuing on to Pomfret, Connecticut, and then to the Committee of Safety, arriving on April 29 in Cambridge. On April 30, Arnold wrote a letter that claimed that there were hundreds of cannons and sundry ammunition at Fort Ticonderoga. He was also provided one hundred British pounds of money, plus powder and balls. On May 2, a subcommittee was appointed to confer with Arnold. On May 3,

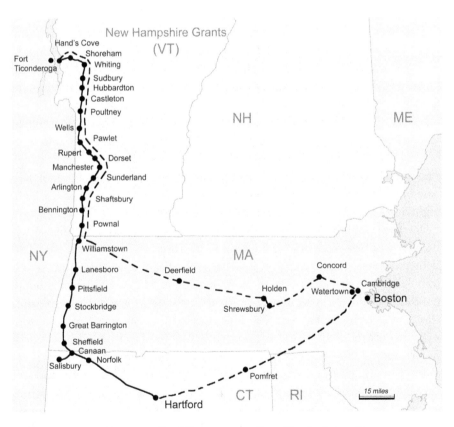

BENEDICT ARNOLD'S ROUTE TO FORT TICONDEROGA. From Hartford, Arnold went east to the Cambridge area and then west to Williamstown, Massachusetts. Then he used the same route as the main expedition to go to Hand's Cove.

FRARY HOUSE, DEERFIELD, MASSACHUSETTS. Built in the 1750s, the Frary House (the left portion) is adjacent to the Barnard Tavern. Benedict Arnold met with Thomas Dickinson (commissary) at the Frary House on May 6, 1775, and then traveled Albany Road (across the street) to Williamstown and on to Fort Ticonderoga.

Arnold was commissioned a colonel and commander over a body of men "not to exceed 400." The Committee of Supplies issued instructions to Deputy Commissary of Supplies Thomas W. Dickinson of Deerfield to purchase fifteen thousand pounds of beef for the men to be raised by Colonel Arnold. He left Cambridge on May 4 with his servant and then went to Concord, where he "dined" and lodged that night at Shrewsbury; he breakfasted in Holden and then ferried across the Connecticut River at Deerfield.

In Deerfield, Massachusetts, he came to the "tavern" of Major Saleh Barnard on the morning of Saturday, May 6, where he breakfasted and sent for Dickinson to give him the request for provisions. Saleh Barnard's place is now the Frary House in Deerfield. Committee of Safety member Colonel David Field was now the new father-in-law of Thomas W. Dickinson, which might account for his being appointed commissary.

Deerfield was full of Tories, and it is amazing that Arnold didn't give away the plan. Just two years prior, a conference of Tories was held in Deerfield at Lieutenant Seth Caitlin's tavern, less than one-fifth of a mile down the road from Saleh Barnard's place. Even more recently, in March 1775 (just about a month before Arnold was here), the "Tory" prisoners from the Westminster Massacre were housed at Seth Caitlin's place on the way to a Northampton prison twenty miles to the south; apparently, "several Deerfield Tories visited the prisoners." The Sons of Liberty had set up a Liberty Pole about three houses from Saleh Barnard's, but local Tories sawed it through the middle. On May 5, apparently, John Graves, a Berkshire Tory, was in Northampton with the news "that a few people from Connecticut had joined a number of Pittsfield people and were gone up to Ticonderoga in order to take it." Nothing came of it, but Deerfield is just north of Northampton.

Just after meeting with Dickinson, Arnold left Deerfield on May 6 for Williamstown (the Albany road is just in front of Saleh Barnard's house).

Dickinson in turn left Deerfield the next day, Sunday, May 7, with his fourteen-year-old brother, Consider. He traveled 130 miles and arrived on May 12 with about fifteen oxen in Castleton, two days too late. The patriotic Dickinson brothers are well known in Deerfield, as Consider's wife donated money for the Dickinson High School. It is remarkable that Arnold in his uniform and Dickinson with his cattle were both going west, away from Boston, and didn't raise any suspicion.

In Williamstown, Arnold spent the night of May 6 at Nehemiah Smedley's Tavern (built in 1772), about one mile east of the Williams Inn on Route 2 (Mohawk Trial). In Williamstown, Arnold probably learned of the other expedition. Arnold was next found on May 8 in Rupert, Vermont. He most likely used the same route as the expedition, which had reached Rupert on May 5.

In Rupert, Arnold writes a letter (the original is still extant), dated May 8, "To the Gentlemen in the Lower Towns": "I beg the favor of you, gentlemen, as far down as this reaches, to exact yourselves, and send forward as many men to join the army here as you can possibly spare." "Lower Towns" probably meant down Route 7 to Sheffield. In his letter, he indicates that 150 had gone ahead (he doesn't mention that they are not his men) and then signs the letter "Commander of the Forces."

Upon arriving in Castleton, he was told by Green Mountain Boys and the leaders, including Mott, that they had a commander, Ethan Allen. Arnold's expedition consisted of one person to help with his clothes. The Green Mountain Boys scoffed at Arnold and his "commission." His commission ordered him to raise four hundred people, and he only had a wardrobe servant with him. He was not in Massachusetts. He had done nothing. He had not recruited any of the men. He had not sent men out to guard the roads. He had not sent a spy to the fort. He was almost trying to ruin the mission with his actions. It would later be shown that he overestimated the number of people needed to take Fort Ticonderoga, which could have ruined the mission if they had waited. Arnold spent the night in Castleton and the next morning raced to catch up with Ethan Allen.

Allen's route to Hand's Cove had been thought out. The night before, he had gone north from Castleton on the road that his brother Ira and Remember Baker had built in 1773, through Hubbardton to Wessels (or Wesels or Wiswell) in Sudbury. Then he went on through parts of Whiting on the same road. Then, where it crosses the Crown Point Road, he used that to go to Hand's Cove, which is located north of Fort Ticonderoga. The fort had been built to defend against attacks mainly from the south, and

NEHEMIAH SMEDLEY HOUSE, WILLIAMSTOWN, MASSACHUSETTS. Benedict Arnold stayed at this house the night of May 6, 1775, and then proceeded to try to catch the expedition that was already on its way to Fort Ticonderoga. The house and marker are on Route 2 east of the Williams Inn about one mile.

the area to the north—on the New York and Grants side—was basically uninhabited wilderness. Hand's Cove itself was hidden from view of the fort and had a shallow ravine situated around a stream that limited viewing from the New York side of the lake, in case there were British patrols.

When Arnold confronted Allen, there was trouble. Mott was so concerned that he went immediately to Shoreham to make sure that Allen did not succumb to Arnold's demands. All of the citizen-soldiers, not just the Green Mountain Boys, threatened to club their rifles (this is done when marching) and leave. Arnold's commission didn't mention giving him authority over any mission let alone over people outside of Massachusetts. There was no written agreement available on what transpired between Arnold and Allen. Allen apparently agreed only to have Arnold travel at his "left side." As recently as the Epaphras Bull diary, published in 1948, it is confirmed that Allen did allow Arnold to be on "his left side" on the attack. There is no evidence that Allen ever relinquished command to the pushy Arnold. Allen may have felt that the commission from Massachusetts was in some way helpful—but not enough to relinquish command.

Part III

The Capture of Fort Ticonderoga

THE SCENE IN THE RAVINE

On the evening of May 9, an estimated two hundred to three hundred patriots were crouched down around the small stream in the shallow ravine at Hand's Cove in Shoreham on the eastern shore of Lake Champlain across from Fort Ticonderoga. Hand's Cove (now on the National Register of Historic Places) was the perfect choice for a jumping-off place to go to the fort. It was north of the fort, which lessened suspicion; it had a low ravine in which to hide; and trees blocked the sightline from the fort, which lay to the southwest. As Robert Maguire points out, in all of Shoreham there was only one Tory, William Reynolds, who ever lived in the town, so the chance of a Tory informing the fort was slim. By having the main rendezvous camp located about twenty-five miles back in Castleton for two days, there was no need to really camp in Hand's Cove and use campfires that might give away their position.

Some of the citizen soldiers had traveled more than two hundred miles from Hartford, Connecticut. They had basically been recruited one at a time by word of mouth and not by written letters, which might fall into the wrong hands. They were hoping they had not been discovered on their journey to Hand's Cove. There was no artillery, no wall-climbing equipment, few if any bayonets and no training as a unit. Except for maybe Ethan Allen and Benedict Arnold, there were also no uniforms. The outfits were farmers' or workmen's clothes and buckskin hunting outfits. Weapons were fowling pieces, muskets, rifles and hunting rifles. Except for Ethan Allen and the

HERRICK HOUSE
AT HAND'S COVE,
SHOREHAM, VERMONT.
The view from the
Hand's Cove staging
area in Vermont across
from Fort Ticonderoga;
the force would cross
Lake Champlain in the
distance on May 10,
1775. *Courtesy Vermont
Historical Society.*

Green Mountain Boys, few had the organized paramilitary experience the Boys had in real life keeping New York at bay for five years.

It was a diverse group, bound together by varying degrees of dislike of tyranny. There were at least 3 lawyers, several college graduates (Yale and Harvard were represented), at least 2 doctors, 1 surgeon's mate and a future congressman. Massachusetts may have had more than the generally estimated 40 people. There were probably over 170 Green Mountain Boys..

Agewise, probably more than 50 percent were over thirty years old. The Green Mountain Boys tended to be older than the Sons of Liberty. Many from Connecticut were a little older and had gone to college. The oldest, Asa Douglas, was about sixty, and there were two teenagers, Luke Noble and Nathan Beman. Most would be considered middle-class people trying to make a living for their families on relatively small plots of land or in trades. Large landowners or upper-class people tended to be Tories, with Benedict Arnold at this time the exception. More than 80 percent of them owned land.

There was at least one spy in the group, Noah Phelps, and two ministers, Nehemiah Hoit and James Easton. Brown, Parsons and David Noble seem to have been Minutemen, and at least Benedict Arnold was in the Sons of Liberty. Ethan Allen's mentor, Thomas Young, although not present, was one of the famous Sons of Liberty leaders at the Boston Tea Party. The Green Mountain Boys, by definition, were almost a combination of Minutemen and Sons of Liberty. The Green Mountain Boys were the militia in the Grants area and were always ready. The spreading of information about their cause and using harassment and "twigs of the wilderness" were tactics of the Green Mountain Boys that were similar to the Sons of Liberty activities such as tarring and feathering in Massachusetts and Connecticut.

Although only about sixty of the two to three hundred were living in Connecticut or Massachusetts at the time, over 90 percent of the entire group had some tie to Connecticut and Massachusetts. There were also many family groups that, in turn, had ties to the Allen clan. There were at least five pairs of fathers and sons, at least three sets of brothers-in-law and the largest immediate family comprised John Roberts and his five sons. The Allens were the largest family group with four brothers and two cousins. Allens were located in many of the towns the expedition visited, such as Pittsfield, Sheffield, Pawlet, Poultney and Castleton. As captains of the Green Mountain Boys, Herrick, Warner, Marvin and Cochran had known one another for years. Many had ties to one another via Salisbury and northwest Connecticut towns. Many would have expenses later reimbursed from the State of Connecticut or other sources.

There were at least two future Tories in the group: Benedict Arnold and Levi Allen, Ethan's brother. Some had brothers who were Tories, and the expedition stayed at a tavern whose owner's brother was a Tory.

Connecticut had brought the money, someone with the guts to be a spy and the chairman of the Committee of War. Massachusetts had brought the second-largest group and, as it turned out, the boats.

The Green Mountain Boys were not a "mob," as Governor Tryon and Lieutenant Governor Colden kept stating. Mobs can't start with one person and grow to more than two hundred people after moving two hundred miles in secret. There was an elected leader, Ethan Allen, who had the respect of all present. They were on a single mission. All were fighting tyranny of some sort—some religious tyranny, some tyranny over the use of their land and some tyranny over the conduct of their lives. Freedom cuts across all walks of life, and this diverse group had a love of freedom.

All of them had to have concerns. Ethan Allen and others were convicted felons in the eyes of New York and could be put to death without the benefit of clergy if caught. Had the fort been warned and the cannons filled with grapeshot ready to mow them down? Would they lose all of their land if there was a settled peace and the Crown ruled in favor of New York?

Where Are the Boats?

Of all the planning Allen and the leaders designed—with guarding the roads, arranging for a guide, sending in a spy to the fort, carefully recruiting loyal people who would not give information to the British and choosing a safe route more than two hundred miles long from Hartford across three colonies—Allen may have ruined the entire mission because, as time went on into the morning of May 10, there were no boats with which to cross the lake. Allen would later make the understatement that "it was with the utmost difficulty I procured the boats to cross the lake." For Ethan Allen to say that, it was clear that this could have been a disaster. It was only three weeks prior at Lexington and Concord that the British had been delayed two hours leaving Boston because of a shortage of boats, which gave the colonists critical time to warn the countryside. Would the same fate happen to Allen?

With daylight approaching, there was still no sign of Herrick from Skenesborough to the south. Had he been captured? Was he just late? Had there been no boats there? The last hope was the backup Asa Douglas (Hancock), who had been sent north toward Panton, Bridport or Crown Point to procure boats. While the group was waiting in Shoreham, Douglas had gone to get a boat belonging to "Mr. Smith." To this end, Douglas stopped to procure the aid of Mr. Chapman. While the two men were talking about getting boats, tradition indicates that two young men, James Wilcox and Joseph Tyler, overheard the conversation. They devised a scheme of their own to acquire a large oar boat owned by Major Skene that lay off Willow Point opposite Crown Point (there are two Willow Points). They roused four more people, so it became a party of six. They decoyed the commander with rum and the ruse that they needed to go to a hunting party that was waiting for them. The captain and his two men were made prisoners. Douglas arrived back in Hand's Cove in a bateau about the same time but a little earlier than Wilcox and Tyler.

Even with this well-organized surprise attack, boats still could have been Allen's downfall. Epaphras Bull from the coastal colony of Connecticut specifically refers in his diary to the boat that took the first group over as a "battoe," which would have been capable of handling forty people. A colonial "battoe" (bateau) was a very specific type of scow with double ends. Because it is a work boat and was sort of the pickup truck of the colonial period, Allen probably thought that it would not be that difficult to find some along the eastern shore of Lake Champlain. He didn't have time to build one, although as the original "instant boats" some could be built in a week along the shoreline. To try to acquire the Fort Ticonderoga ferryboat (which was actually running in 1759, probably on an unorganized basis, and the boat was probably just a canoe or small rowboat then) was too risky

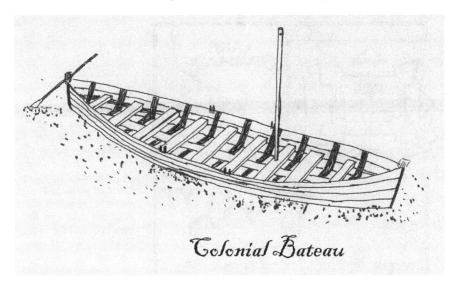

Colonial Bateau

COLONIAL BATEAU ("BATTOE"). The common bateau was a specific double-ended scow averaging about thirty feet in length and designed for inland and shallow waters. It was the "pickup truck" of the colonial period, used for hauling people, cargo and more. The first forty people to cross Lake Champlain to capture Fort Ticonderoga used a bateau.

given that it was in sight of Fort Ticonderoga. Allen was lucky. To bring a thirty-foot bateau (or other boat capable of handling forty people) south from Bridport meant going up Lake Champlain, which flows north, and is no simple task.

Nevertheless, in the early morning of May 10, they had transportation. Forty people in the bateau headed across the lake. From Hand's Cove, they went south past what is now Larrabee's Point (the Fort Ticonderoga–Larrabee's Point ferry leaves from this point) about a mile and then southwest across the lake; they landed just north of Willow Point. There they waited for the boat to return with another group of people. In one and a half hours, two boats returned. Allen stated years later, "I landed 83 men." It is not clear if he included himself in this number. The irony is that Asa Douglas, who got the boats, was not in the group.

After sending the boats back for more people, Allen realized that by the time the boats returned the sun would be up. If he waited, he would lose the surprise of daylight (most of the Green Mountain Boys' successful surprises on unsuspecting "Yorker" settlers took place at night). He made the decision to try to take the fort right then with the eighty-three men he had landed. There were some reports that there was also another confrontation here with Arnold about command. In any event, the agreement made on the

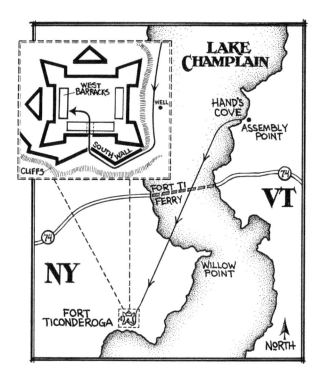

MAY 10, 1775. HAND'S COVE TO FORT TICONDEROGA. Boats left Hand's Cove and landed on the beach north of Willow Point. The citizen soldiers then marched about half a mile to the fort past Pontleroy's redoubt, the East Wall and the well and then went through a breach in the south wall to the Wicket Gate. Then they went through the sally port (main entrance) and climbed to the second floor of the south end of the west barracks to Captain Delaplace's quarters.

Hand's Cove side of the lake did not change. Arnold would be on Allen's "left side." Allen was still in command.

"AMERICA'S FIRST VICTORY" ON MAY 10, 1775

As Allen himself said when he described the venture, "It was viewed hazardous" and as a "desperate attempt." Therefore, Ethan Allen lined up the troops in three ranks and, in his account of that night, gave a pep talk involving his dislike of "arbitrary power":

> *Friends and fellow soldiers, you have for a number of years past been a scourge and terror to arbitrary power. Your valor has been famed abroad, and acknowledged as appears by the advice and orders to me from the General Assembly of Connecticut to surprise and take the garrison before us. I now propose to advance before you, and in person, conduct you through the wicket gate; for we must this morning either quit our pretentions to valor, or possess ourselves of this fortress in a few minutes; and, inasmuch as it is*

The Capture of Fort Ticonderoga

SOUTH WALL, FORT TICONDEROGA, TICONDEROGA, NEW YORK. This is a picture of the restored fort today. In 1775, the walls were stone, but the height at the parapets was probably not as great, and there were some breaches in this outer wall. *Photo by Nathan Farb. Courtesy Fort Ticonderoga.*

a desperate attempt, which none but the bravest of men dare undertake, I do not urge it on any contrary to his will. You that will undertake voluntarily, poise your fire-locks.

Since Allen was still about half a mile from the fort itself, hidden behind trees on the beach, he could reasonably have given this pep talk, although maybe not in a booming voice all could hear. Allen himself was now on New York land and, if caught, the royal governor who favored the Tories could execute him.

It was now about four o'clock in the morning. Allen ordered the men to face right, and at the head of the center file, he marched them toward the wicket gate. As shown on Thomas Jeffreys's map, the more eastern road went through wooded areas that had not been cleared, a condition that would afford more cover. From the beach north of Willow Point, Allen, with Nathan Beman's help, took the eastern road leading past the charcoal oven, the Pontleroy redoubt and the well, skirting the east wall of the fort to the ruined entrance at the south wall. Just opposite this break in the center of the south curtain of the fort, there was a large gate with a smaller wicket gate within the bigger gate.

At the wicket gate, Allen found a sentry, who tried to fire; Allen then chased him through the covered way (it is still there today as the main entrance to the center parade grounds—"Place de Arms"). On the parade grounds, Allen lined up his troops to face the two barracks (west and south) and gave three "Huzzas," which surprised the garrison. One of the sentries made a pass at one of the "officers" (Easton), but Allen deflected the attack with his sword and then demanded that the sentry take him to the commanding officer's headquarters. The sentry pointed to the southern door on the second floor of the west barracks. Allen later said that the commander, Captain William Delaplace, came to the door with his breeches in his hand. In response to the question of under whose authority Allen demanded surrender, Allen said:

In the name of the Great Jehovah and the Continental Congress.

Reports later from the second in command, Lieutenant Feltman, indicate that it was Feltman to whom Allen made his famous statement. However,

ETHAN ALLEN'S CAPTURE OF FORT TICONDEROGA. The original painting in 1848 was by Alonzo Chappel and depicts Ethan Allen and the British commander. Ethan Allen was guided to the fort by a youth, Nathan Beman. *Courtesy National Archives.*

Allen's statement is still interesting because the Second Continental Congress had not even met yet (it was scheduled to meet in a few hours in Philadelphia). Furthermore, Allen's relationship with the "Great Jehovah" is mysterious given Allen's religious views.

The Green Mountain Boys and the entire contingent of eighty-three stormed into the Place de Arms and rounded up about sixty-eight people in the British garrison, which also included twenty-four women and children. Most prisoners would be taken to Hartford. Much to the distress of Benedict Arnold, the Boys opened some of the twenty-four kegs of rum. As Allen once said, as only Allen could, "We tossed about the flowing bowl" and wished success to Congress and to the liberty and freedom of America. Arnold would later claim that Allen was good at leading his own "wild" men but no one else. However, Allen, in one of the bizarre incidents of the war, gave Captain Delaplace a receipt for the rum, which the State of Connecticut later honored: "To Capt. Delaplace, for liquors supplied 18 [pounds], 11 [shillings] 9 [pence]."

It was over in probably less than ten minutes. The "Gibraltar of the Americas" was now in American hands—five years after the Green Mountain Boys had been organized because the king would not decide the land issue with New York. No one had been killed on either side in the capture of Fort Ticonderoga nor had the Green Mountain Boys killed anyone in the five years of battling New York.

By morning, the total number of people who had crossed Lake Champlain and entered the fort was over four hundred, according to some accounts. Allen sent Seth Warner off the next day with one hundred men to take His Majesty's Fort at Crown Point (about fifteen miles to the north) with its twelve men. This was done; about one hundred more cannons were captured, and now the Americans were basically in control of Lake Champlain. Remember Baker, who had been summoned previously, came down the lake and prevented two British boats from Crown Point from going to Canada to warn of the loss of the forts.

The Spoils

Benedict Arnold (and some others) compiled an accounting of the material captured and their condition:

Table 3. Arms captured at Fort Ticonderoga (report dated May 11, 1775).

3	18-pounders, good
2	French pounders, bad
2	12-pounders, good
6	12-pounders, double fortified, good
2	12-pounders, useless
12	9-pounders, good
5	9-pounders, bad
18	6-pounders, bad
9	4-pounders, good
1	16-pounder, good
19	swivels, good
2	wall pieces, good
2	French 12-pounders, bad
1	13-inch mortar and bed, good
1	7-inch mortar and bed, good
1	7-inch howitzer, good
86	cannons
28	iron truck wheels
10	carriages
42	port fires
17	ladles
17	linstocks
100	18-pound shot
550	12-pound shot
240	9-pound shot
1,430	6-pound shot
168	quilted grapeshot
9 tons	lead balls
3,700 pounds	iron balls
28 barrels	powder, damaged
906	shells
30,000	flints

Note: In the list, which gives the condition of some of the cannons (some bad but serviceable), there are no twenty-four-pounders or others listed. Some cannons were apparently on the edge of the lake, and their conditions were not known. Other lists, without indication of

The Capture of Fort Ticonderoga

condition, are as high as 120 cannon and 50 swivels. Another report adds that there was also "a warehouse full of material for boat building" and "10 casks of very indifferent powder." Arnold also didn't count the foodstuffs or the rum. None of the cannons had been indicated as having been "spiked" or made useless.

Disaster Averted and Success Achieved

Not having Fort Ticonderoga warned about a surprise attack seemed to be a miraculous combination of skill and luck. The expedition had sent people to Albany, New York, with its many Tory sympathizers, to discover the temper of the people but no one sent word to Fort Ticonderoga. The growing body of recruits was moving through many towns with Tories or Tory sympathizers. Some people on the expedition or their families themselves had Tory leanings. Benedict Arnold had proposed his plan to the Committee of Safety in Cambridge and Dr. Benjamin Church was on that committee and was convicted for communicating with the British General Gage less than three months later. Arnold also had Thomas Dickinson drive cattle through the countryside from Deerfield to feed his potential recruits. The British themselves had been sending information to Fort Ticonderoga but it never arrived in time.

Without the capture being a surprise, there could have been a large loss of life and perhaps even failure. The powder, whether "damaged" or "indifferent," was not useless. At least one sentry tried to fire his gun, so he knew that he had enough powder (although perhaps the flint caused the misfire). Also, there was enough powder around for Matthew Lyon to fire in celebration the large thirteen-inch mortar known as "Old Sow." There appears to have been enough powder, flint and grapeshot for at least some of the nine four-pounders. Even dated French and Indian War four-pounders loaded with fifteen to twenty musket-sized balls were capable of killing twelve people in one blast. If the British had been warned, they could have also sifted and dried even more powder.

Allen had attacked with only eighty-three men. The four-pounders and smaller cannons could easily have been moved by some of the forty-two enlisted men in front of any wall breaches or inside the fort itself. The reports weren't clear as to exact size of the "swivels" captured, but these cannons were designed to be rotated, and some were very light and could be lifted by one man. Ticonderoga was a fortress with some "broken walls and gates" but was by no means wholly indefensible, especially against a group of only eighty-three men.

FORT TICONDEROGA CANNONS, FORT TICONDEROGA, NEW YORK. Even smaller cannons than these, if armed with grapeshot (i.e. musket balls), could kill more than twelve men in one blast or send a four-pound ball more than two thousand feet, which is more than enough to hit a boat in Lake Champlain.

The other boats still had not come back from Hand's Cove with the remaining people, so they could have been subject to bombardment or repulsing at the shore. Even the smaller four-pounder cannons could hurl a four-pound ball two thousand feet—almost half a mile.

Perhaps equally important, there was no indication that any cannons or supplies were "spiked" to make them unusable to colonists. The members of the garrison at the fort also could have set fire to boat-building supplies or even the powder. With warning, they could have set fire to the powder, spiked the guns and gone north and done the same to the cannons at the fort at Crown Point. No one even had time to leave to warn that British fort fifteen miles away.

It appeared that the warnings the expedition received from the people at Rupert and that Brown received on the way to Bennington were accurate-in a way. Apparently, Lieutenant Feltman had come down from Canada to reinforce the fort about April 29, but he was with only about ten people

The Capture of Fort Ticonderoga

"AMERICA'S FIRST VICTORY" MARKERS, SHOREHAM, VERMONT. The Hand's Cove chapter of the DAR marker is on the left. The more recent Lake Champlain Basin marker is on the right. In the far distance across from Lake Champlain is Fort Ticonderoga.

and had not heard about Lexington and Concord. Guarding the roads also prevented news of Lexington and Concord from reaching Fort Ticonderoga.

"America's First Victory," less than three weeks after Lexington and Concord, had been accomplished by keeping secret the mustering of two to three hundred citizen militia, some from two hundred miles away in Hartford, Connecticut. With secrecy, speed and trust, they were able to surprise the British.

John Brown was sent to the Continental Congress in Philadelphia with the British flag. Some prisoners were sent to Hartford. Seth Warner took a contingent north and captured His Majesty's Fort at Crown Point the next day.

In retrospect, if the Crown had ruled quickly and decisively on the status of the existing landowners in the Grants, there probably never would have been the need for the creation of the Green Mountain Boys. Instead, the Crown never made its "wishes known" and therefore created this more than two-decade-long struggle for the land titles between the colony of New York and the colony of New Hampshire.

Lieutenant Governor Colden—who was in charge of New York in the absence of Governor Tryon and who was of course very sympathetic to the Tory cause—embarrassingly wrote to the British minister Lord Dartmouth in England with his apologies: "The only people of this province [New York] who had any hand in this expedition were that lawless people who whom your lordship has heard much of under the name of the Bennington Mob." This was not entirely true, as there were New Yorkers in the expedition.

AFTERMATH AND HISTORIC TRIVIA

The morale of the colonists increased dramatically. The "Gibraltar of the Americas" had fallen to citizen militia. Fort Ticonderoga would remain in the Americans' hands for two more years, until July 6, 1777, when the British recaptured it on their march toward Saratoga. By capturing Fort Ticonderoga, America controlled Lake Champlain, and this bought time to allow for the build-up of defenses and organiztion in the colonies.

In the winter of 1775–76, Henry Knox took many of the cannons from Fort Ticonderoga and Crown Point to Boston at the request of George Washington. Fearing bombardment from the American cannons placed on Dorchester Heights, the British evacuated Boston Harbor on March 17, 1776. Today this is celebrated as Evacuation Day in Suffolk County, which includes Boston.

Ethan Allen went to Canada on a military expedition in 1775, was captured and spent the next two and half years in a prison in England, but he was returned and freed under a prisoner exchange. The war had moved south, but Allen was still active in revolutionary efforts. In 1787, Allen moved to Burlington, Vermont, and died in 1789 at the age of fifty-one. A painting of Ethan Allen was never commissioned.

The "New Hampshire Grants" area became New Connecticut in January 1777. In July 1777, it became Vermont and for the next fourteen years was an independent republic with its own militia, coins, postal system and constitution. On March 5, 1791, after fourteen years, Vermont became the fourteenth state, the first after the original thirteen. Ethan Allen never knew Vermont as a state in the United States.

SETH WARNER MEMORIAL AND GRAVE SITE, ROXBURY, CONNECTICUT. Ethan Allen's cousins, Seth Warner and Remember Baker, were born in Roxbury. (Some claim that Ethan Allen was also born there.) Seth Warner, after twenty years in Vermont, returned to Roxbury because of illness and died there.

Benedict Arnold went on to help the American cause at the Battle of Valcour Island and at the Battle of Saratoga. Ironically, it was Samuel Holden Parsons, who had met Arnold outside Hartford, who became a general and in 1778 established West Point as a "permanent military post." In 1780, Benedict Arnold became a traitor and tried to turn over West Point to the British. Arnold moved to England and died there.

The Allen clan owned an estimated 120,000 acres in Vermont by 1791, four times greater than the next largest landowner, Thomas Chittenden, the governor. The land owned by the Allen clan comprised a lot of what is the Burlington area today. Ira Allen donated the land for the University of Vermont

Seth Warner went on to be a hero at the Battle of Bennington and then returned to Roxbury, Connecticut, because of illness. He died there at the young age of forty-one. Route 30 from Manchester to Middlebury is named after him.

Left: SETH WARNER MEMORIAL HIGHWAY. Route 30 North from Manchester (site of this marker) to Middlebury has been designated the Seth Warner Memorial Highway. Major parts of this route were used in the capture of Fort Ticonderoga. Warner was one of the commanders during this event.

Below: 1955 COMMEMORATIVE U.S. POSTAGE STAMP. This U.S. commemorative stamp depicts Ethan Allen and Fort Ticonderoga with its distinctive four-bastion star-shape layout. The cannons and powder cask (barrel) were of the type captured by Ethan Allen's forces. *U.S. government stamp.*

The Capture of Fort Ticonderoga

USS *ETHAN ALLEN*. The first in the Ethan Allen class of nuclear submarines, this submarine had sixteen missile tubes. It was used in the film *The Hunt for Red October*, and in 1962 it fired the only nuclear-armed Polaris missile ever launched. Built at the Electric Boat Division of General Dynamics in Groton, Connecticut, the USS *Ethan Allen* was commissioned on August 8, 1961, and decommissioned on March 31, 1983. *U.S. government photo.*

Remember Baker, Allen's cousin, went to Canada and was killed by Indians and buried in Canada—the first American to die in Canada.

James Easton dedicated his life to the American cause but died poor.

The United States issued a Fort Ticonderoga commemorative stamp in 1955.

Two U.S. warships were named after Ethan Allen. The second, the USS *Ethan Allen*, was part of the Ethan Allen class of submarines that included the USS *Thomas Jefferson*.

John Montressor, the chief British engineer in North America, wrote a report noting that Fort Ticonderoga should be reinforced. He had a daughter, Frances Montressor ("Fanny"); in 1784, she married Ethan Allen. Fanny's stepfather was Crean Brush, one of the New Yorkers who put out the reward for Ethan Allen.

King George III was born in 1738 and became king of the British empire at twenty-two years old in 1760. Ethan Allen was born in 1738 and at twenty-two was drifting between occupations and trying to support his brothers and family members in 1760.

Several notable firsts resulted from the expedition: America's first victory, America's first prisoners and the first surrendering of the flag over the king's property. As Matthew Lyon said when he fired the mortar in celebration, it was the first cannon shot fired under the auspices of the American eagle. Seth Warner's capture of the fort at Crown Point was America's second victory.

Statuary Hall in the Capitol rotunda in Washington features two statues from each state: one statue from Vermont is of Ethan Allen; one statue from New Hampshire is of John Stark, who was involved in building Crown Point Road, used in part by Allen to capture Fort Ticonderoga; one statue from Massachusetts is of Samuel Adams, who had sent John Brown to Canada (who, in turn, suggested that the Green Mountains Boys should capture it); one statue from Connecticut is of Roger Sherman, one of the delegates to the Continental Congress along with Silas Deane (who had signed the loan to pay for the Ticonderoga expedition); the other Connecticut statue is of Jonathan Trumbull, who was a close personal friend of Christopher Leffingwell, who also signed the receipt for the money to capture Fort Ticonderoga; and the statue from New York is of Robert R. Livingston, who was the son of Judge Livingston, who ruled the New Hampshire titles invalid, thus leading to the creation of the Green Mountain Boys.

Appendix I

General Timeline

1609: Champlain explores south into what would become Lake Champlain, and Hudson explores north up what would become the Hudson River. Soon, 150 years of territory disputes will begin in the Champlain Lake Valley and Hudson River Valley.

1749: Benning Wentworth, governor of New Hampshire, starts granting town charters for the unsettled area now known as Vermont. The area is also claimed by New York. His first town of the New Hampshire Grants west of the Connecticut River is Bennington.

1755: The French build Fort Carillon (Fort Ticonderoga) on Lake Champlain, the "Gibraltar of the Americas."

1758: The British attack Fort Carillon with 16,000 troops and are repelled by only 3,500 French troops.

1759: The British again attack Fort Carillon, but it is abandoned by the French, who move north to protect Canada. The British renamed Fort Carillon as Fort Ticonderoga and reinforce it. The British build Crown Point Road running from New Hampshire across what is now Vermont to Lake Champlain.

1759–60: Quebec and Montreal fall. The French and Indian War ends. Eastern America is now British.

Appendix I

1761: The chartering of towns and settlement of the New Hampshire Grants increases rapidly—settlers mainly come from Connecticut and Massachusetts.

1763–75: Resentment of British rule intensifies in the New England colonies. The Green Mountain Boys are formed to fight New Yorkers trying to assert their claims. Sons of Liberty and Minutemen are also formed.

1775 (April 19): Battles of Lexington and Concord April 19—the shot heard 'round the world. The rebellion is on.

1775 (April 28): A small group in Hartford leaves to go north to ask the Green Mountain Boys to capture Fort Ticonderoga. More patriots are recruited in Connecticut and Massachusetts.

1775 (May 5): In Bennington, Ethan Allen agrees to command a secret expedition and marches north recruiting Green Mountain Boys en route.

1775 (May 9): In Castleton and Shoreham, Benedict Arnold tries to take command of the more than two hundred men massed at Hand's Cove, Vermont, in preparation for the attack.

1775 (May 10): Eighty-three men cross Lake Champlain and execute a surprise attack. More than one hundred cannons are captured.

1775 (May 11): Seth Warner leads the capture of Crown Point, fifteen miles north of Fort Ticonderoga.

1776 (March 17): The captured cannons from Fort Ticonderoga are placed on Dorchester Heights above Boston Harbor, and the British evacuate the harbor. This is celebrated today as Evacuation Day in Suffolk County.

1776 (July 4): The thirteen colonies declare independence from England.

1777: The Grants formally declare independence with the name New Connecticut. The name is changed to Vermont, which operates as an independent republic with its own coins, constitution, militia, postage system and so forth for fourteen years until it joins the other thirteen states as the fourteenth state in 1791.

Appendix II

Longitude and Latitude Coordinates for GPS Users

Global Positioning System (GPS) coordinates eliminate issues with houses burning down or being moved, names changing, changes in appearance, markers being moved and so on. For privacy, these GPS coordinates come from public places. Accuracy is based on consumer GPS systems. Also, Crown Point Road Association gives GPS coordinates for each of the markers on the old road. These selected points are described in the text. Please respect privacy.

Location	Latitude	Longitude

CONNECTICUT

Salisbury

Location	Latitude	Longitude
Ethan Allen Furnace Salisbury	N 41° 57' 47"	W 73° 26' 27"

Canaan

Location	Latitude	Longitude
Lawrence House	N 42° 1' 24"	W 73° 19' 28"

Litchfield

Ethan Allen Birthplace/Home 149 Old South Street	N 41° 44' 5"	W 73° 11' 18"

New Haven

Arnold House Site 155 Water Street	N 41° 18' 5"	W 72° 5' 19"

Roxbury

Seth Warner Grave Memorial	N 41° 33' 24"	W 73° 18' 32"

MASSACHUSETTS

Deerfield

Frary House	N 42° 32' 40"	W 72° 36' 16"
Albany Road	N 42° 32' 37"	W 72° 6' 7"
Wilkinson property	N 42° 33' 8"	W 72° 36' 11"
Caitlin Tavern site	N 42° 3' 27"	W 72° 36' 20"

Sheffield

Dan Raymond House	N 42° 6' 40"	W 73° 21' 10"

Stockbridge

Red Lion Inn	N 42° 56' 73"	W 73° 18' 45"

Williamstown

Nehemiah Smedley House	N 42° 42' 28"	W 73° 11' 31"

Longitude and Latitude Coordinates for GPS Users

Fort West Hoosac	N 42° 42' 50"	W 73° 12' 39"

Pittsfield

Easton Tavern Marker	N 42° 51' 73"	W 73° 15' 4"

Watertown

Edmund Fowle House	N 42° 22' 7"	W 71° 10' 48"

Cambridge

Hastings House/ Committee of Safety marker	N 42° 22' 36"	W 71° 7' 9"
William Dawes marker	N 42° 22' 32"	W 71° 7' 10"

VERMONT

Old Bennington

Catamount Tavern site	N 42° 53' 6"	W 73° 12' 49"
Ethan Allen Homesite marker	N 42° 53' 2"	W 73° 12' 47"
Warner Homesite	N 42° 54' 37"	W 73° 15' 12"
Samuel Herrick Homesite	N 42° 52' 38"	W 73° 15' 29"
Jewett House	N 42° 51' .5"	W 73° 12' 10"

Shaftsbury

David Galusha Tavern	N 42° 58' 54"	W 73° 12' 24"
Robert Frost House	N 42° 56' 4"	W 73° 12' 35"

Arlington

Hawley-Crofut House	N 43° 4' 33"	W 73° 9' 56"

Tory Lane	N 43° 4' 31"	W 73° 9' 44"
Remember Baker mill plaque	N 43° 3' 35"	W 73° 8' 21"

Sunderland

Ira Allen House	N 43° 6' 53"	W 73° 7' 22"

Manchester

Weller Tavern	N 43° 9' 20"	W 73° 4' 23"
Dellwood Cemetery	N 43° 9' 15"	W 73° 4' 30"
Original Marsh Tavern site	N 43° 9' 42"	W 73° 4' 19"

Dorset

Ethan Allen Spring	N 43° 14'	W 73° 5' 30"
Kent Meadows	N 43° 14' 11"	W 73° 5' 50"

Pawlet

Blossom Corner	N 43° 24' 5"	W 73° 13' 33"

Castleton

Richard Bentley's Farm marker	N 43° 36' 43"	W 73° 10' 33"
Zadock Remington Tavern site	N 43° 36' 32"	W 73° 11' 23"

Rutland

Meads Tavern Site marker	N 43° 36' 6"	W 73° 1' 18"
Green Mountain Boy DAR statue	N 43° 36' 27"	W 72° 58' 19"

Longitude and Latitude Coordinates for GPS Users

Whiting

Beach Marker	N 43° 51' 52"	W 73° 12' 2"
Samuel Beach Home	N 43° 51' 15"	W 73° 12' 41"

Shoreham

Hand's Cove (from water)	N 43° 51' 43"	W 73° 22' 23"

Burlington

Winooski (Onion) River	N 44° 29' 18"	W 73° 11' 12"
Ethan Allen family graves	N 44° 29' 3"	W 73° 11' 13"

Poultney

Heber Allen grave site	N 43° 31' 39"	W 73° 12' 2"

NEW YORK

Fort Ticonderoga	N 43° 50' 20"	W 73° 23' 17"
Ethan Allen gate area	N 43° 50' 29"	W 73° 23' 16"

Appendix III

Arnold's Role

There was no written agreement between Arnold and Allen. There seems no question that Arnold was at the side of Allen—and more precisely, the "left side." Therefore, he was in front, which is leading the expedition. Some have misinterpreted this "leading" as "commanding." Almost all written documents (diaries, letters and more) from the colonists and the Massachusetts Committee of Safety point only to Ethan Allen as the sole commander. Even biographies about Arnold written in conjunction with descendants indicate that Arnold was allowed to be on the expedition as a volunteer, with no command authority even over Massachusetts patriots. The most recent 1948 Bull diary confirms previous statements that Arnold claimed command, but "however agreed he take the left side"

Only Arnold's letters and one other letter written by a mysterious "Veritas" (attributed to Arnold) imply that Arnold was part of some joint command. One writer in 1928, Allen French, feels that Arnold had joint command based primarily on one of the British officers (Feltman) indicating that he had heard Arnold and Allen say that they were in command. However, Feltman's letter was written thirty days after the event, and the letter contains other mistakes. Also, French's book was written before Epaphras Bull's diary was published.

Arnold's regimental command book seems to indicate failure at taking command. References to clubbing and going home if Arnold were to command came not just from the Green Mountain Boys but from everyone. Mott, the chairman of the Committee of War, says in writing the next day that Allen was commander. After the capture, members of a Massachusetts fact-finding committee reported that they "do not find that he had any under his command at the time of the reduction of these fortresses."

Arnold made some very patriotic efforts later in the war at Valcour Island and at Saratoga, but it seems hard to conclude that he did anything more than volunteer at Ticonderoga. A good starting point for exploring this issue further would be the fourth volume of *The Bulletin of the Fort Ticonderoga Museum*, published in January 1937. L.E. Chittenden goes into detail about why Arnold was not in command, and the more recent Bull diary supports his analysis.

Appendix IV

Selected Related Historic Sites

B esides the specific sites mentioned, here are some places open to the public.

Fort Ticonderoga National Historic Landmark
Ticonderoga, New York
www.fort-ticonderoga.org
Museums, cannons, tours and other daily activities in season.

Carillon Cruises
Larrabees Point, Vermont
www.carilloncruises.com
Views from Lake Champlain of Hand's Cove, from which Ethan Allen left, and of Fort Ticonderoga; excellent narrative of the events in 1775 and other years (plus sonar).

Crown Point Road
www.crownpointroad.org
Good maps allow for the exploring/hiking of the two-hundred-mile-long road.

Red Lion Inn
Stockbridge, Massachusetts
www.redlioninn.com
The expedition to capture Fort Ticonderoga stopped here.

Mount Defiance
Ticonderoga, New York
Spectacular views of Vermont (Hand's Cove) and Fort Ticonderoga give a strategic sense of events.

Bennington Battle Monument State Historic Site
Bennington, Vermont
www.historicvermont.org
The 306-foot-tall monument, built in 1891 to celebrate the Battle of Bennington, is on the original road Ethan Allen took on his march north. Visitor's Center and elevator inside the monument. There is also a view of the Vermont Valley, showing the route to Ticonderoga.

Bennington Museum
Bennington, Vermont
www.benningtonmuseum.org
The museum has many artifacts from the Catamount Tavern and other sites.

Ethan Allen Homestead
Burlington, Vermont
www.ethanallenhomestead.org
In the last two years of his life, Ethan Allen lived in this house. Some of the Green Mountain Boys were in the Burlington area when they received the call to meet at Fort Ti. The Allen clan developed this entire region from 1773, which accounts for Ethan Allen's visits to the area from southern Vermont.

Frary House
Deerfield, Massachusetts
www.historic-deerfield.org
The house at which Benedict Arnold stopped on the way to Fort Ticonderoga. Tours are given.

Edmund Fowle House
Watertown, Massachusetts
www.historicwatertown.org
Various key committees met here, and the Provincial Congress met nearby.

Selected Related Historic Sites

Williams Inn
Williamstown, Massachusetts
www.williamsinn.com
The site of the westernmost fort protecting Massachusetts, located near the
Nehemiah Smedley Home, where Benedict Arnold stayed on May 6 on the
way to Fort Ticonderoga.

Lake Champlain Maritime Museum
Vergennes, Vermont
www.lcmm.org
Replica *Perseverance*, a colonial bateau. The museum also does considerable
research on the types of boats used, and it really is the authority on maritime
Lake Champlain.

Simsbury, Connecticut:
The Simsbury Historical Society, at 800 Hopemeadow, maintains the Elisha
Phelps House, and just up the road, at 731 Hopemeadow Street, is the 1820
House sited on land once owned by Noah Phelps. Simsbury Cemetery,
where Noah Phelps is buried, is a short walk from 800 Hopemeadow.

Appendix V

Participant Details

As the expedition moved north, there were many with ties back to Connecticut, so it is important to establish those who lived in Connecticut at the time. The most quoted figure for people on the expedition living in Connecticut at the time is sixteen, but it appears that there were more than this. In his journal, Edward Mott from Connecticut writes, "We collected to the number of sixteen people in Connecticut." In the first volume of the collections of the Connecticut Historical Society, seventeen men from Connecticut are listed as being in the expedition. Those who left Hartford with Mott (they were unarmed) are shown with an asterisk:

Edward Mott	*John Stevens*
Levi Allen	*Elisha Phelps*
Samuel Blagden	*Noah Phelps*
Epaphras Bull*	*Bernard Romans*
Elijah Babcock*	*Josiah Stoddard*
Gershom Hewitt	*Jeremiah Halsey**
Ezra Heacock	*William Nichols**
Ashbel Wells	*John Bigelow**
Thomas Barber III	

However, Robert O. Bascom, in his list compiled in the late 1800s and early 1900s, indicates four others who were associated with Connecticut: Samuel H. Parsons, Simeon Belding (Hartford), Elias Herrick (Hartford) and Samuel Keep (Salisbury). Parsons has been associated with Middletown and not Massachusetts as Bascom indicates. This would give a total of twenty for Connecticut. Heman Allen is widely associated with Salisbury (because of his general store), but neither the Connecticut or Bascom lists have him as being from Connecticut. If he is included with Connecticut, then the total becomes twenty-one. In Bull's diary, he indicates a somewhat unknown Asa Eddy, "joined from Salisbury," although Bascom does not have a town for him. If he is added to Connecticut, the number becomes twenty-two. Romans, who is included, started from Connecticut but left the expedition later, so those at Ticonderoga from Connecticut at the time would be back to twenty-one. Changes could also occur depending on classification of whether some individuals from Connecticut were actually living in Connecticut at the time. This would apply to Heman Allen and Samuel Keep. The latter may have been living in Crown Point at the time.

General Notes

1. The Epaphras Bull diary was first published by the Fort Ticonderoga Museum in its 1948 bulletin and again in 1977. It is the only known contemporary diary written by someone on the trip. As such, when compared to some nineteenth- and twentieth-century works it helps to fill in gaps in previous texts.

2. There have been some accounts that it was not Samuel Beach but rather his father Gershom (born 1729) who made the infamous recruiting trip of more than sixty miles in less than twenty-four hours. It could be that both were involved in the ride. Since Ethan Allen was friends with Gershom, it could have been he who started the ride, but then his son finished. In Pittsford, reports have stated that Beach recruited Benjamin Cooley, who was Beach's brother-in-law. Since Samuel Beach's sister, Ruth, married Benjamin Cooley, it could have been Samuel who went from Pittsford to Shoreham. The Vermont Chapter of the National Society Daughters of Founders and Patriots of America put the "Paul Revere" marker up in 1956 in Whiting for Samuel Beach. In Boston, Paul Revere and William Dawes started the famous ride, but Dr. Prescott actually reached Concord.

3. It would appear that Arnold may have visited Watertown, which is adjacent to Cambridge. The Provincial Congress had met there, and some of the documents involving Arnold indicated Watertown as opposed to Cambridge.

4. Tradition suggests that Litchfield is Ethan Allen's birthplace, but some have claimed Roxbury (part of Woodbury at the time). The birthplace home in Litchfield is now a private residence at 149 Old South Road.

5. Based on expense reports, times, dates and distances, it would appear that Heman Allen may have actually started his express run to Bennington from farther south (Salisbury) rather than from Pittsfield. Based on some reports, he may have actually left from Hartford, where he may have been on Onion River Land Company business. The important fact seems to be that Heman Allen was sent ahead, and Ethan Allen and the leaders in Bennington had at least one day or so to discuss whether to help in the capture of Fort Ticonderoga.

6. In the late nineteenth and early twentieth centuries, after many years of research, Robert O. Bascom of Fort Edward, New York, developed a list of the individuals on the expedition. After additions over the years, the list now indicates by name 128 of the estimated 200 to 300 who were with the expedition, and 53 of the 83 who crossed Lake Champlain and entered the fort are also indicated by name. The list is available in several places, including on the Ethan Allen Homestead website (www.ethanallenhomestead.org). The list should be read carefully. Notice that there is no heading for the "town" column. Also, not all Bascom lists are identical. This town reference sometimes means where the person is from, sometimes where the person lived at the time and sometimes where the person lived after May 10, 1775. Here are some comments on key people shown on the list, starting with Josiah Stoddard:

- Josiah Stoddard is listed in Salisbury, Connecticut records as a volunteer on the expedition and is also listed in the Connecticut Historical Society records as being on the expedition. However, he is not listed by Bascom. Serious consideration should be given to adding him to Bascom's list.

Here are comments on other people on the Bascom list:

- Ethan Allen lived in Bennington from 1769 to 1775.
- Gideon Warren is indicated as being from Hampton, New York, but was more associated with Pownal.
- Samuel H. Parsons is from eastern Connecticut, not Massachusetts.
- Remember Baker was living in Colchester about May 10, 1775.

- Enos Flanders is listed as Sheffield, Vermont, but there is no record of such a Vermont town being granted.
- Samuel Beach moved to Whiting after the Revolutionary War.
- Benjamin Cooley was in Pittsford, Vermont, about May 10.
- Asa Douglas's farm is more accurately in Stephentown, New York, today; Jericho changed its name to Hancock.
- Peleg Sunderland lived in Manchester and Rutland, Vermont.
- Samuel Poppleman and Epaphras Bull do not appear on some Bascom lists.
- Samuel Keep is listed as being from Salisbury, Connecticut, but Salisbury does not list him. He is believed to have moved to Crown Point, New York, about 1773.

7. Goodhue in *History of Shoreham* notes that Allen's party after leaving Castleton "directed their way to the old Crown Point Road." Goodhue apparently had spoken with some descendants who had said that Allen then pursued the old Crown Point Road "through Whiting into Shoreham." Since Crown Point Road's Ticonderoga branch splits off in Sudbury and goes west through Orwell, this would indicate that Allen went north and then west on the main Crown Point Road through Whiting to Shoreham. The various routes of the old Crown Point Road are still being explored and identified today. See www.crownpointroad.org.

8. Military ranks changed frequently, but I have tried to use the rank most commonly associated with that individual. For ease of reading, Vermont and the "Grants" are used interchangeably, although there was no true "Vermont" until 1777. There are a variety of spellings of some names and places, but again the most common are used for clarity. Captain Delaplace spelled his own name in different ways. Skenesborough can also be Skenesboro. Road routes should be treated as "corridors" since in many cases portions of roads have changed. Since towns are large (in Vermont they are generally six miles by six miles), historical references to going through a town does not always mean the center of town. For instance, the Crown Point Road did not go through the center village of Whiting. Distances from town to town vary because it would depend on where in the town the distance is being measured from, so distances should be considered estimates. For town population estimates in 1775, I used Bellesiles's numbers because they were collected on the same basis, so they can be used more for comparative purposes. They were also collected for the year of interest, 1775. For the New England colonies in 1770, I used the U.S. Census Bureau estimates.

9. Many of Ethan Allen's claims of what he said were written several years later.

10. Jeremiah French Sr. is generally believed to have purchased the land in Manchester, but it was his son Jeremiah French Jr. who lived in Manchester and Dorset and became a Tory. Many times, land was purchased but not officially recorded until years later

11. Vermont town charter lists sometimes vary due to the granting of partial towns or rechartering or granting of special military charters.

Bibliography

Aldrich, Lewis Cass. *History of Bennington County, Vermont.* Syracuse, NY: D. Mason and Company, 1889.

Allen, Ethan. *The Narrative of Colonel Ethan Allen.* Cambridge, MA: Applewood Books, 1989.

Allen, Ira. *The Natural and Political History of the State of Vermont.* Rutland, VT: Charles E. Tuttle Publishers, 1969.

Arnold, Benedict. Regimental Memorandum Book Written While at Ticonderoga and Crown Point. Reproduced with comments. *Pennsylvania Magazine of History and Biography* 8 (1884).

Atlas and Gazetteer Vermont. 12th ed. Yarmouth, ME: DeLorme, 2007.

Beach Family magazine.

Bellesiles, Michael A. *Revolutionary Outlaws: Ethan Allen and the Struggle for Independence on the Early American Frontier.* Charlottesville: University of Virginia Press, 1993.

Borman, Lauri D. *Atlas of American History.* Skokie, IL: Rand McNally, 2005.

Bort, Mary Hart. *Manchester Memories of a Mountain Valley.* With the assistance of the Manchester Historical Society. Tucson, AZ: Marshall Jones Company, 2005.

Brown, Charles Walter. *Ethan Allen of Green Mountain Fame.* Chicago, IL: M.A. Donohue and Company, 1902.

Bulletins of the Fort Ticonderoga Museum, 1937–1988. Fort Ticonderoga, New York.

Burditt, Claire, and Sylvia Sullivan. *Castleton: Looking Back the First 100 Years.* Rutland, VT: Castleton Historical Society, 1998.

Burgoyne, John, Lieutenant General. *A State of the Expedition From Canada as Laid Before the House of Commons*. London: J. Almon, 1780.

Captain John Warner's Green Mountain Rangers. www. greenmountainrangers.com.

Caverly, A.M., MD. *History of the Town of Pittsford, Vermont*. Rutland, VT: Tuttle & Company, 1872.

Chapin, Carl M. *Manchester in Vermont History*. Manchester, VT: Manchester Historical Society, 1932.

Chartrand, Rene. *Ticonderoga 1758: Montcalm's Victory Against All Odds*. Oxford, England: Osprey Publishing, 2000.

Cheney, Cora. *Vermont: The State with the Storybook Past*. Shelburne, VT: Second New England Press, 1996.

Child, Hamilton. *Gazetteer and Business Directory of Bennington County for 1880–1881*. Syracuse, NY: Journal Office, 1880.

Chipman, Daniel. *Memoir of Colonel Seth Warner*. Panton, VT: Essence of Vermont, 2000.

Chittenten, Lucius E. *The Capture of Ticonderoga with Appendix (Containing Original Letters)*. Rutland, VT: Tuttle & Company, 1872.

Clark, Cameron. The White Pine Series Architectural Monographs. Vol. 8, no. 5. *Houses of Bennington Vermont and Vicinity*. St. Paul, MN: White Pine Bureau, 1922.

Coffin, Charles C. *The Boys of '76*. Gainesville, FL: Maranatha Publications, 1998.

Coffin, Howard, Will Curtis and Jane Curtis. *Guns over the Champlain Valley*. Woodstock, VT: Countryman Press, 2005.

Coleman, Emma Lewis. *A History and Present Day Guide to Old Deerfield*. Norwood, MA: Plimpton Press, 1907.

Collections of the Connecticut Historical Society. Vol. 1, *1860: Papers Relating to the Expedition to Ticonderoga April and May*. Hartford: Connecticut Historical Society, 1775.

Collections of the Vermont Historical Society. Vol. 1. Montpelier, VT: Printing and Publishing Committee, 1870.

"Col. Seth Warner's Extra-Continental Regiment." www.warnersregiment.com.

Commanger, Henry Steele, and Richard B. Morris. *The Spirit of Seventy-Six: The Story of the American Revolution as Told by Participants*. New York: First Da Capo Press, 1995.

Congdon, Herbert Wheaton. *Old Vermont Houses*. New York: Alfred Knopf, 1946.

Connecticut Quarterly 4 (January–December 1898).

Cook, Flavius J. *Home Sketches of Essex County: Ticonderoga.* Keeseville, NY: W. Lansing and Son, 1858.

Crannell, Karl. *John Stark: Live Free or Die.* Stockton, NJ: OTTN Publishing, 2007.

Crego, Carl. *Fort Ticonderoga.* Charleston, SC: Arcadia Publishing, 2004.

Crockett, Walter H. *Soldiers of the Revolutionary War Buried in Vermont.* Excerpted from *Proceedings of Vermont Historical Society 1903–04, 1905–*06. Baltimore, MD: Genealogical Publishing, 1973.

Crown Point Road Association. *Historical Markers on the Crown Point Road.* Rutland, VT: Crown Point Road Association, 2004.

Daughters of the American Revolution. Families Allied with the Green Mountain Boys as Recorded in Lineage Books of the Charter Members. Washington, D.C.: Daughters of the American Revolution, n.d.

Davis, Kenneth S. "In the Name of the Great Jehovah and the Continental Congress." *American Heritage* 14, no. 6 (October 1963): 65–77.

Davis, William, and Christina Tree. *The Berkshire Hills and Pioneer Valley of Western Massachusetts.* Woodstock, VT: Countryman Press, 2004 and 2007 second edition.

De Puy, Henry W. *Ethan Allen and the Green Mountain Heroes of '76.* New York: Phinney and Blakeman, 1861.

Dorset Historical Society. *Walking and Driving Tours of Dorset Vermont.* Dorset, VT: Dorset Historical Society, 2004.

Dorset Vermont Bicentennial, Map and Legend. George A. Russell Collection of Vermontiana. Canfield Library, Arlington, Vermont, n.d.

Duckworks magazine. The "Rooster's" Tale. www.duckworksmagazine.com.

Duffy, John J., Ralph H. Orth, J. Kevin Graffagnino and Michael Bellesiles. *Ethan Allen and his Kin.* Vol. 1. Hanover, NH: University Press of New England, 1998.

Dunning family. Genealogical notes on the Dunning family in America. Compiled and printed June 25, 1915, New York Public Library.

Eggleston, H. *Equinox House Driving Map-Manchester, Vermont.* Chester, VT: National Survey Company, 1892.

Farrington, Charles C. *Historic Cambridge Common.* Bedford, MA: Bedford Printing Shop, 1918.

Filson, Brent. "The Warm and Winsome Walloomsac Inn." *Vermont Life* (Summer 1984): 8–11.

Fitchbury Railroad Company. "Williamstown: The Berkshire Hills and Thereabout." Glens Falls, NY: C.H. Possons, 1890.

Force, Peter. American Archives. Series Four, 1840. CD, 9 vols., LeGrand J. Weller, 2009.

Foulke, Patricia, and Robert Folk. *A Visitors Guide to Colonial and Revolutionary New England*. Woodstock, VT: Countryman Press, 2006.

French, Allen. *The Taking of Ticonderoga in 1775: The British Story*. Cambridge, MA: Harvard University Press, 1928.

Fritz, Jean. *Traitor*. New York: Putnam and Grosset Group, 1997.

Goodhue, Josiah F., Reverend. *History of the Town of Shoreham*. Shoreham, VT: A.H. Copeland, 1861.

Graffagnino, J. Kevin. "Representations of a Turbulent Land, Some Vermont Maps, 1755–1798." *Rutland Historical Society Quarterly* 12, no. 1 (Winter 1982).

———. *The Shaping of Vermont*. Rutland: Vermont Heritage Press, 1983.

Graffagnino, J. Kevin, and H. Nicolas Muller III. *The Quotable Ethan Allen*. N.p., n.d.

Gustafson, Peter. "A Lost Hero of the Green Mountain Boys: Remembering Remember Baker." *Bulletin of the Fort Ticonderoga Museum* 15, no. 1 (Winter 1988): 15–28.

Hahn, Michael T. *Ethan Allen: A Life of Adventure*. Shelburne, VT: New England Press, 1994.

Hall, Henry. *Ethan Allen: The Robin Hood of Vermont*. New York: D. Appleton and Company, 1895.

Hall, Hiland. "Historical Readings." *State Banner*, 1841–42.

———. *History of Vermont from its Discovery to its Admission into the Union in 1791*. Albany, NY: Joel Munsell, 1868.

Hall, S.R. *The Geography and History of Vermont*. Revised by Pliny White. Montpelier, VT: C.W. Willard, 1871.

Hamilton, Edward P. *Fort Ticonderoga: Key to a Continent*. Fort Ticonderoga, NY: Fort Ticonderoga, 1995.

Hemenway, Abby Maria. *Vermont Historical Gazetteer: A Magazine Embracing the History of Each Town*. 3 vols. Burlington, VT: self-published, 1868.

Henry, Hugh. *Arlington Along the Battenkill: Its Pictured Past*. Arlington, VT: Arlington Townscape Association, Inc., 1993.

Hibbard, George S. *History of Rupert, 1761–1898*. Rutland, VT: Tuttle & Company, n.d.

Hill, George Canning. *Benedict Arnold: A Biography*. Boston, E.O. Libby and Company, 1858.

Hill, Ralph Nading. *Lake Champlain: Key to Liberty*. Taftsville, VT: Countryman Press, 1977.

Hine, Marie Sheldon. "Collection of Rupert History, March 6, 2006." In *Bennington Museum Vermont Historical Events Guide 2003*. Wilmington, VT: Living History Association, 2003.

Holbrook, Stewart H. *Ethan Allen*. New York: Macmillan Company, 1940.

Holister, Hiel. *Pawlet: 100 Years*. Albany, NY: J. Munsell, 1867.

Houghton, Raymond C. *A Revolutionary Day Along Route 7*. Delmar, NY: CyberHaus, 2001.

Howe, Archibald M. "Colonel John Brown of Pittsfield Massachusetts: The Brave Accuser of Benedict Arnold." An address given in 1908. N.p.: Kessinger Publishing, LLC, 2009.

Jeffreys, Thomas. *A Plan of the Town and Fort of Carillon at Ticonderoga, 1758*. London, England, 1774.

Jellison, Charles A. *Ethan Allen: Frontier Rebel*. Syracuse, NY: Syracuse University Press, 1969.

Jepson, George H. *Herrick's Rangers*. Bennington Museum Series No. 1. Bennington, VT: Hadwen, Inc., 1977.

Jones, Ronald D. *John and Ethan: A Revolutionary Friendship*. Salisbury, CT: Salisbury Association, 2007.

Joslin, J., and B. Frisbie. *The History of Poultney*. Poultney, VT: Poultney Historical Society, n.d.

Journal of Vermont Senate, February 27, 1996.

Journals of each provincial congress of Massachusetts in 1774 and 1775, and of the Committee of Safety with an appendix; published agreeably to a resolve passed March 10, 1837, under the supervision of William Lincoln, Bost Dutton and Wentworth, Printers to the State. N.p., n.d.

Kerle, Phyllis E. *Pittsfield…Where Legends Begin*. Pittsfield, MA: Berkshire Chamber of Commerce, n.d.

Ketchum, Richard M. *Divided Loyalties*. New York: Henry Holt and Company, n.d.

———. *Saratoga*. New York: Henry Holt and Company, 1997.

Kilbourne, Payne Kenyon. *Sketches and Chronicles of the Town of Litchfield, Connecticut*. Hartford, CT: Lockwood and Company, 1859.

Kirby, Ed. *Echoes of Iron in Connecticut's Northwest Corner*. Sharon, CT: Sharon Historical Society, 1998.

Klyza, Christopher McGrory, and Stephen C. Trombulak. *The Story of Vermont: A Natural and Cultural History*. Hanover, NH: University Press of New England, 1999.

Lewis, Phebe Ann. *The Equinox, Est. 1769: Historic Home of Hospitality*. Manchester, VT: Johnny Appleseed Bookshop, 1993.

Lossing, Benson J. *The Pictorial Field-Book of the Revolution*. New York: Harper and Brothers, 1860.

Maguire, J. Robert. "Hand's Cove: Rendezvous of Ethan Allen and the Green Mountain Boys for the Capture of Fort Ticonderoga, Vermont." *Proceedings of the Vermont Historical Society* 33, no. 4 (October 1965): 416–37.

Maynard, Charles W. *Fort Ticonderoga*. New York: Rosen Publishing Group, 2002.

McKnight, Jack. "Ethan Allen, Philosopher." *Vermont Life* (Winter 1990).

McLaughlin, David J. *The Unfolding History of the Berkshires*. Scottsdale, AZ: Pentacle Press, 2007.

Medcalfe, Mr. *A Map of Country in which the Army Under Lt. General Burgoyne Acted in the Campaign of 1777 and the Places of Principle Actions*. Engraved by William. N.p., n.d.

Merrill, John, VDS, and Caroline R. Merrill. *Sketches of Historic Bennington*. Cambridge, MA: Riverside Press, 1898.

Merrill, Perry H. *Vermont Under Four Flags*. Montpelier, VT: Northlight Studio Press, 1975.

Montressor, John. "Montressor Family Papers." Fort Ticonderoga Museum, microfilm.

Mott, Edward. "Journal of Capt. Edward Mott." *Collections of the Connecticut Historical Society* 1 (1860): 163–68.

Munson, Loveland. *The Early History of Manchester: An Address Delivered in the Music Hall on December 27, 1875*. Manchester, VT: Journal Print, 1876.

Neumann, George C. *Battle Weapons of the American Revolution*. Texarkana, TX: Scurlock Publishing, 1998.

Nickerson, Hoffman. *The Turning Point of the Revolution*. Boston: Houghton Mifflin, 1928.

Ninman, Royal R. "Historical Collection from Official Records and Files of Part Sustained by Connecticut during the War of the Revolution." With appendix containing important letters and depositions, written during the war, Hartford, 1842. Charing Cross, London: E. Gleason Faden, 1780.

Onion, Margaret Kent. *Look About Castleton*. Castleton, VT: Castleton Women's Club, 1977.

Page, John. "The Economic Structure of Society in Revolutionary Bennington." *Proceedings of the Vermont Historical Society* 49, no. 2 (Spring 1981).

Parks, Joseph, and the Bennington Museum. *The Battle of Bennington: August 16, 1777*. Bennington, VT: Bennington Museum, Inc., 2004.

Pawlet Becentennial Committee. *A Pictorial Scrapbook*. Pawlet, VT: Pawlet Bicentennial Committee, 1975.

Pell, John. *Ethan Allen*. Boston: Houghton Mifflin, 1929.

Petersen, James E. *Seth Warner: "This Extraordinary American."* Middlebury, VT: Dunmore House, 2001.

Petersen, Max. *Salisbury: From Birth to Bicentennial*. Salisbury, VT: Dunmore House, 1991.

Peterson, Harold. *Encyclopedia of Firearms*. London: E.P. Dutton & Company, 1964.

Phelps, Edward J. *One Day in August 1777*. N.p.: Park McCullough House Association, n.d.

Preiss, Lillian E. *Sheffield, Frontier Town 1733–1976*. Sheffield, MA: Sheffield Bicentennial Commission, 1976.

Randall, Willard Sterne. *Benedict Arnold: Patriot and Traitor*. New York: William Morrow and Company, 1990.

Rebok, Barbara, and Doug Rebok. *History of Bennington County*. Vermont: Plus Printing Company, n.d.

Red Lion Inn. *A History of the Red Lion Inn*. Stockbridge, MA: self-published, 1987.

Rensselaer-Taconic Land Conservancy, Rensselaer County Historical Society and Taconic Valley Historical Society. *Through a Country Not Well Settled: The Albany Road of 1752–1773*. Berlin, NY: self-published, 1999.

Resch, Tyler. *Bennington's Battle Monument: Massive and Lofty*. Bennington, VT: Images from the Past, 1993.

———. *Dorset: In the Shadow of Marble Mountain*. For the Dorset Historical Society. West Kennebunk, ME: Phoenix Publishing, 1989.

———. *The Shires of Bennington*. For the Bennington Museum. Bennington, VT: Bennington Banner, 1975.

Risch, Erna. *Supplying Washington's Army*. Washington, D.C.: Center of Military History, United States Army, 1981.

Rogers, Stillman D., and Barbara Radcliffe Rogers. *Country Towns of Vermont*. Lincolnwood, IL: Country Roads Press, 1999.

Rose, Ben Z. *John Stark: Maverick General*. Waverly, MA: TreeLine Press, 2007.

———. "Molly Stark's Cannon." Amazon Short, 2007.

Ross, John. "The Saga of Gentleman Johnny Burgoyne." *Vermont Life* 29, no. 2 (Winter 1974): 44–45.

Rudd, Malcolm Day. *The Men of Worth of Salisbury Birth*. Salisbury, CT: Salisbury Association, Inc., 1991.

Sage, James D. "The Old Topping Tavern." *Vermont Life* 25, no. 3 (1971): 42–47.

Salisbury Association, Inc. "Town of Salisbury." Vols. 1 and 2. Salisbury, CT: self-published, 1913.

Shalhope, Robert E. *Bennington and the Green Mountain Boys*. Baltimore, MD: Johns Hopkins University Press, 1996.

Sheldon, George. *A History of Deerfield Massachusetts*. Vol. 2. Facsimile of the 1895–96 edition. Published in collaboration with the Pocumtuck Valley Memorial Association. Somersworth, NH: New Hampshire Publishing Company, 1972.

Sheldon, Henry Rupert, MD. Dictated oral history.

Sherman, Michael, Gene Sessions and P. Jeffrey Potash. *Freedom and Unity: A History of Vermont*. Barre, VT: Vermont Historical Society, 2004.

Shy, John. *Toward Lexington: The Role of the British Army in the Coming of the American Revolution*. Princeton, NJ: Princeton University, 1965.

Smith, Donald A. "Legacy of Dissent: Religious Politics in Revolutionary Vermont 1749–1784." PhD dissertation, Clark University, n.d.

Smith, H.P. and W. S. Rann. *History of Rutland County, Vermont*. Syracuse, NY: D. Mason & Company, 1886.

Smith, J.E.A. *The History of Pittsfield from the Year 1734 to the Year 1800*. Boston: Lee and Shepard, 1869.

Smith, Justin H. *Our Struggle for the Fourteenth Colony: Canada and the American Revolution*. Vol. 1. New York: G.P. Putnam's Sons, 1907.

Spargo, John. *Ethan Allen at Ticonderoga*. Rutland, VT: Tuttle & Company, 1926.

Sparks, Jared. *The Life of Colonel Ethan Allen*. Burlington, VT: C. Goodrich and Company, 1858.

State of Vermont, Division of Historic Preservation. *Historic Sites and Structures Survey*. Montpelier, VT: State of Vermont, Division of Historic Preservation, n.d.

Steele, Joseph, Reverend. "An Abridged History of Castleton, Vermont." In *Vermont Historical Gazetteer*. Vol. 3. Burlington, VT: Abby Hemenway, 1877.

Stoll, Ira. *Samuel Adams: A Life*. New York: Free Press, 2008.

Stout, Marilyn. "Vermont Walks: Village and Countryside." *Vermont Life* (1995).

Swift, Samuel. *Statistical and Historical Account of the County of Addison, Vermont*. Middlebury, VT: A.H. Copeland, 1859.

Symonds, Craig L. *A Battlefield Atlas of the American Revolution*. Mount Pleasant, SC: Nautical and Aviation Publishing Company of America, Inc., 1986.

Thompson, D.P., Judge. *The Green Mountain Boys*. Weybridge, VT: Cherry Tree Books, 2000.

USS *Ethan Allen* (SSBN 608). U.S. Navy. http://navysite.de/ssbn/ssbn608. htm.

Vermont Historical Society archives. Vermont History Center. Barre, Vermont.

Vermont Historical Society. *Barre/Montpelier.* Barre: Vermont Historical Society, 2005.

Vermont History, no. 1 (Winter 1974).

Vermont History 24, no. 2 (April 1956).

Wallace, Audrey. *Benedict Arnold: Misunderstood Hero?* Shippensburg, PA: Burd Street Press, 2003.

Walton, E.P., ed. *Records of the Council of Safety and Governor and Council of the State of Vermont, July 1775–1777.* Vol. 1. Montpelier, VT: J. and J.M. Poland, 1873.

Webster, Harold, and Elizabeth Webster. *Our Whiting.* Includes 1800 map of Whiting by Harold Webster. Rutland, VT: Academy Books, 1976.

Weeks, John M. *History of Salisbury, Vermont.* Middlebury, VT: A.H. Copeland, 1860.

Whitelaw, James A. *Correct Map of the State of Vermont from Actual Survey.* Montpelier, VT, 1976.

Wilbur, James Benjamin. *Ira Allen: Founder of Vermont, 1751–1814.* Vol. 1. Boston: Houghton Mifflin, 1928.

Williams, Samuel. *The Natural and Civil History of Vermont.* Vol. 2. Burlington, VT: Samuel Mills, 1809.

Wolfe, Virginia A., and Mary Bort. *Manchester Village, Vermont: Walk on Marble to Points of Interest.* Manchester, VT: Manchester Historical Society, n.d.

Works Progress Administration for the State of Vermont, Federal Writers Project. *Vermont: A Guide to the Green Mountain State.* Cambridge, MA: Houghton Mifflin, 1937.

Index

Index

About the Author

R ichard Smith's travels throughout the world spurred an appreciation and interest in history. This fascination with history led to his creating historical maps and self-guided history tours that have been published and distributed throughout the Northeast. Dick's previous book, *The Revolutionary War in Bennington County: A History & Guide*, has been on several bestseller lists. He earned degrees in engineering and management from Lehigh University and an advanced degree in economics from Columbia University. He is a trustee of the Vermont Historical Society and former president of the Manchester Historical Society. He resides in Manchester, Vermont, with his wife, Sharon. He also hosts a TV show on New York and Vermont history.